New Vegetarian Basics

New Vegetarian Basics

NETTIE CRONISH

RANDOM HOUSE OF CANADA

Canadian Cataloguing in Publication Data

Cronish, Nettie, 1954–
    New vegetarian basics

ISBN 0-679-30978-0

I. Vegetarian cookery. I. Title

TX837.C763 1999   641.5'636   C98-932552-0

Cover and interior design: Sharon Foster Design
Cover photograph: Vince Noguchi
Illustrations: Susan Todd

Printed and bound in the United States of America

0 9 8 7 6 5 4 3 2 1

To my mother, Mrs. Helen Cronish,
and my aunt, Mrs. Jenny Nainudel,
who have both guided
and supported me all my life.

CONTENTS

Acknowledgments

One cold rainy night in March 1997, I was on my way to a Cuisine Canada dinner at a reputable restaurant. As I walked through the door, Anita Stewart (former director and founder of Cuisine Canada) took me by the elbow and said that she wanted me to meet someone. That someone turned out to be David Kent, President and Publisher of Random House of Canada. After Anita introduced me (with a lot of enthusiasm and praise for my work), David turned to me and asked whether I could write a vegetarian cookbook that would be stimulating and precise—and that's how this cookbook came to be written.

As I took my seat later that evening, I was already planning this book. The restaurant (they claim) never received my faxed request for a vegetarian meal, so as I sat there munching away on my third plate of organic greens, I knew I had to write a book that could be of use to everyone: vegetarians, nonvegetarians wishing to add more vegetarian meals to their diet, vegans, food professionals, home cooks and finally the old-fashioned curious. Anita's generosity of spirit had connected me to the right person, then, lots of hard work and support from Random House encouraged me to do the best job that I could. So I would like to say thank you, David and Anita.

Heartfelt thanks to everyone at Random House of Canada, and to Doug Pepper, a visionary of vegetarian cuisine. Thanks also to Sharon Foster, the art director who made the book so attractive; Beverley Renahan, recipe editor; Barbara Selley RD, and Beverley Bell-Rowbotham of Info Access (1988) Inc. for their excellent nutritional analyses; photographer Vince Noguchi and food stylist Ettie Shuken for the beautiful cover; and to Alex Beveridge for my photograph.

Thanks to the Big Carrot healthfood store, Karma Co-op, the Ontario Natural Food Co-op and the Toronto Women's Culinary Network who have given me a great deal of professional support over the years. And to my wonderful recipe testers who have gold-plated taste buds, Laura Buckley and Kate Gammal. Numerous colleagues have offered valuable moral support and practical advice: Jocie Bussin, Rhonda Caplan, Marilyn Crowley, Naomi Duguid, Daphna Rabinovitch and Theresa Taylor. Special thanks to Barbara Barron, Gabriele Sousa Machado Costa, Ruth Gayle, Liz Greisman, Laurie Malabar and Eve Weinberg.

For love, patience and a clean kitchen, I thank my handsome husband Jim Urquhart, my children Cameron and Mackenzie and my cousin Suzie Siegal.

INTRODUCTION

People choose to eat a vegetarian diet for various reasons—spiritual, nutritional, ecological, political and social. I became a vegetarian because I got transferred from the fields to the kitchen on the Israeli kibbutz I was living on. Rather than be part of a large group of cheesecake makers, I chose to assist the vegetarian chef—her precondition was that I be vegetarian. So, overnight and overweight, I began examining more carefully what I was eating, especially where calories came from. When I returned from globe-trotting, I invested in a food scale that allowed me to measure out the amount of food I was eating. Within a year I shed those 25 extra pounds and felt better than I ever had eating a nonvegetarian diet.

The word vegetarian has two parts: "veget" and "arian." "Veget" means to enliven or bring to life. The second part, "arian," means believer or advocate, someone who will defend a cause or argues on behalf of someone. I don't see myself as a defender of vegetables, but I do believe in the virtue of not eating meat. The question I get asked a lot by many of my cooking class students and others is: What exactly is "meat"? Does fish count? How about foods that animals produce such as eggs or milk and milk products?

Within the vegetarian community, there is a lot of debate and discussion over what vegetarians should and should not eat. Today, vegetarians generally fall, with some crossover, into three categories. An ovolacto vegetarian eats eggs and milk products. Lacto vegetarians eat milk products but no eggs. Vegans refrain from eating any animal products and also avoid wearing or using products made from animals, such as leather shoes, down comforters, honey and beeswax candles. Then there are people who don't fit into any of these categories, people who eat fish or chicken but no red meat, people who call themselves casual or semi-vegetarians. My own brand of vegetarianism has evolved over time. I used to include dairy products but with the years, and as a result of my husband's lactose intolerance, I've gradually decreased my use of them.

In the past we vegetarians have often felt the need to justify our decision to eat a vegetarian diet. But times have changed and vegetarian cookbooks no longer need to prove their point. My goal for *New Vegetarian Basics* is not to teach you how to eat vegetarian but how to cook vegetarian meals. Once you've learned what is involved in eating a healthy balanced vegetarian diet that supplies you with all your nutritional requirements, often the next question is how do I cook more vegetarian dishes? Learning how to use soyfoods, grains, beans and sea vegetables as the focal ingredients in vegetarian dishes is just like using chicken, beef or lamb in nonvegetarian dishes—and just as easy!

I haven't forgotten what it is like to want to make changes but not have enough of the right information. I do hope this cookbook will help make people cook delicious and nutritious vegetarian meals with confidence. But it's also just as important to know *what* you are shopping for as well as knowing how to cook it. Confronted by seven kinds of tofu to choose from at your local health food store? After you've read the New Vegetarian Basics section you will know how to choose, use, store and cook tofu as well as many other vegetarian staple ingredients.

The recipes have been tested twice (some three times) and include preparation and cooking times as well as nutritional analyses to assist you when meal planning. Many recipes can be doubled in quantity then frozen for future meals. You'll find I've used both old-fashioned and cutting-edge ingredients and techniques throughout the recipes. Simple explanations of ingredients can also be found in the Glossary.

Whatever your food orientation, *New Vegetarian Basics* encourages you to try new products and ingredients that are exploding onto the shelves of local health food stores and even supermarkets. The Natural Foods Pantry section (page 15) will help you stock up on items you'll need to cook the dishes in this book. When you are buying new and unfamiliar ingredients, buy them in small amounts to discover first if you like the taste and texture. As you familiarize yourself with the ingredients, you can start combining favourite ones in exciting new ways.

For many people, eating a plant-centred diet is the dawn of a new way to eat. Meals that don't include meat can require a little extra planning but they don't have to be complicated. The pleasure of eating a delicious vegetarian meal is a satisfying experience and one that can be easily achieved. With easy-to-prepare, appetizing recipes and an understanding of what the vegetarian basic ingredients are and how to shop for them, you'll be cooking sumptuous vegetarian dishes in no time. Whether you are a veteran vegan or a meatless Monday type, *New Vegetarian Basics* has a lot to offer.

NUTRIENT VALUES

Info Access (1988) Inc. of Don Mills, Ontario performed nutrient analysis of the recipes using the nutritional accounting system component of CBORD Menu Management System. The nutrient database was the 1997 Canadian Nutrient File supplemented when necessary with documented data from reliable sources.

The analysis was based on:

- imperial measure and weight (except for foods typically packaged and used in metric quantity) and
- first ingredient listed when there was a choice.

Calcium-fortified soy milk (300 mg calcium per cup/250 mL) and firm tofu containing 162 mg calcium per 100 grams were used in the analysis. Optional ingredients and ingredients in unspecified amounts (including pinches of salt) were not included in the analysis.

Recipe nutrient values were rounded to the nearest whole number; excellent and good sources of calcium, iron, folacin and vitamin C were also identified. Please refer to the accompanying chart for Recommended Daily Intakes of these minerals and vitamins, and for minimum levels per serving supplied by excellent and good sources. You will notice that small portions (e.g. tablespoon/15 mL of dressing) are not excellent or good sources; like the other recipes, they contain nutritious ingredients but not enough per portion to reach excellent or good source levels.

Calcium	Iron	Folacin	Vitamin C

Recommended Daily Intakes* ("RDIs")*

Calcium	Iron	Folacin	Vitamin C
1100 mg	14 mg	220 mcg	60 mg

Excellent source provides at least:

25% RDI			50% RDI
275 mg	4 mg	55 mcg	30 mg

Good source provides at least:

15% RDI			30% RDI
165 mg	2 mg	33 mcg	18 mg

*Reference standards for Canadian nutrition labelling (*Guide to Food Labelling and Advertising, March 1996* and amendments, Canadian Food Inspection Agency)

THE NEW
VEGETARIAN BASICS

———

This is where it all begins. Whether I shop at the local farmer's market, health food store or supermarket, having a house full of fresh, delicious ingredients inspires me to cook, sometimes several meals at a time. Being organized in the kitchen is half the battle. The other half is having the best possible ingredients to create culinary masterpieces. So wipe down your shelves, clear a section of your refrigerator, here come the vegetarian basics. The following sections describe the ingredients I frequently use to create vegetarian meals. Once you've learned what they are and how to cook them, it won't be long before you start making up dishes of your own.

THE HUMBLE SOYBEAN

I find it very ironic that the soybean, one of North America's biggest export cash crops, is used mostly for animal feed (hogs, cows and chickens) and rather than consuming soybeans through soybean-based foods, we eat the animals that eat the soybeans. But I do believe there will be a soyfood revolution! New food technologies have created many uses for the illustrious soybean, ranging from milks, ice creams, sauces, cheeses and nuts.

I use three major soyfoods in many of my recipes: tofu, tempeh and miso. These soyfoods are sources of good-quality protein, and they are free from cholesterol and low in saturated fat.

Tofu

You could say that tofu has a mild, unimposing taste. In other words, don't eat tofu unless you marinate it or combine it with more flavourful ingredients. According to legend, tofu was discovered in China about 2,000 years ago when someone accidentally curdled soy milk in sea water. People acknowledged tofu's importance as a source of protein and its use spread. It was introduced in Japan in the eighth century by Buddhist monks and it gradually developed into the consistency of a more delicate, firm custard, as opposed to the dense, dry Chinese variety. Over the centuries, tofu has become a staple of Japanese cooking. It is only in the last 20 years or so that it has gained popularity in vegetarian communities.

To make tofu, soybeans are soaked, drained and ground. The ground beans are simmered in water, strained and pressed until dry to produce soy milk. A coagulant is then added to the soy milk to cause curds to form. The curds are poured into tofu-pressing boxes (perforated for drainage of the whey) and pressed or weighed down until the curds take shape and become firm. The tofu is then stored in water in the refrigerator.

Storing Tofu

Tofu that you buy as loose cakes or in plastic tubs should be immersed in water in a covered container and refrigerated. Use it within a week to ten days, or according to the expiry date on the package. If you find yourself stuck with leftover tofu, freeze it. I make a vow at the beginning of my cooking classes that no one need ever throw out an expired piece of tofu! (Check the Tofu Minestrone on page 61.) In a perfect world, people would change the water of stored tofu every day. Every other day is fine. Vacuum-packed tofu need not be opened and stored in water. It will keep unopened for a month, or until expiry date. Once opened, it should be stored and used the same as loose tofu.

When you buy prepackaged tofu, carefully read the label. It should contain the following list of ingredients: organic soybeans, water, coagulating agent calcium chloride or magnesium chloride (a coagulating agent is used to curdle soy milk into tofu, as rennet is used to curdle milk into cheese), nutritional information such as fat, protein and calories, and an expiry date. You should always rinse tofu in cold water for a few minutes when it is removed from the package. Health food stores sell firm pieces in a bucket or small container.

Pressing Tofu

Pressed tofu, or *extra firm* tofu, is firm tofu that has been pressed to reduce its water content. This makes it more absorbent so it can readily take on flavours from marinades. Some of my recipes contain pressed tofu. It's my favorite take-along for a picnic salad. It can be easily tossed and will not crumble, and can even masquerade as feta cheese. Follow these instructions to make your own pressed tofu:

Slice the cake of tofu in half in uniform thickness so that the tofu will press evenly. Select two plates of the same size. Place two layers of clean cloth napkins, dish towels or paper towelling on the bottom plate. Place the slices of tofu on top of the napkins, then another layer of napkins on top of the tofu. Place the second plate on top. Select a suitable 5 lb (2.2 kg) weight (I use the base of my food processor). Place weight on top of plate. Press for 30 minutes, near the sink for easy draining.

Freezing Tofu

Leftover tofu? No problem. Freezing tofu changes its soft texture to a chewy meat-like (ground chuck) coarse ingredient. Freezing also increases tofu's spongelike ability to absorb the flavours of ingredients or spices with which it's cooked. When thawed, its new, porous, highly absorbent texture will retain the flavours even more readily than fresh tofu, making it useful for marinating. Thawed tofu will not crumble as easily as fresh and is excellent in soups, stews, casseroles and sauces. Its chewy texture makes it more appealing than regular tofu to a lot of beginners. Tofu's colour changes as it freezes: it turns amber when frozen and later fades to a light beige.

To freeze tofu, remove it from the water, cut it into four slices and wrap each tightly in plastic wrap. Then seal them in plastic freezer bags. Individual packaging will allow you to remove pieces as desired. For best results, freeze it for at least 12 hours before using. The tofu can be frozen for a maximum of six months. Any longer and its texture becomes too tough and dry.

Frozen tofu must be defrosted before using. Remove all plastic wrap and place tofu in a deep bowl, cover with boiling water and let stand for 10 minutes, then drain. Rinse with cool water, then press firmly between your palms to expel all moisture. You will be able to press more water from it if you squeeze it like a sponge. Thawed tofu should be as dry as possible.

Tempeh

A high-protein soy food, tempeh is made by fermenting crushed cooked soybeans which have been inoculated with the bacteria *Rhizospirus oligosporus*. It resembles a spongy, flat slab that's mottled with small black and grey spots, and its texture is very different from tofu. Tempeh can be steamed, fried, braised, crumbled and poached. It is now being made from soybeans and grains (millet, brown rice and quinoa) and is usually sold frozen. Fresh or defrosted tempeh will keep for five days in the fridge. Tempeh can be frozen for a maximum of six months.

You must cook tempeh thoroughly and never eat it uncooked because it can cause digestive upsets. Here is why: Tempeh is a slab of cooked soybeans bound together by a white mycelium, much the same as Camembert or Brie cheese. Like yogurt, tempeh is a cultured food. It is made by the controlled fermentation of soybeans. The bacterial culture is mixed with the partially cooked soybeans, then spread out in flat sheets about ½ inch (1 cm) thick and incubated at 88°F (31°C) for 32 hours. The beans are then bound by the mould into firm cakes. The fermentation process enhances the flavour, and the enzymes from the mould break down the complex proteins, fats and carbohydrates of the soybeans, making them easier to digest. The only way to deactivate the bacterial culture, the culprit in stomach upsets, is to cook the tempeh. Once cooked, it can be left in the fridge for five days and leftover tempeh can be frozen.

To cook tempeh:
Steam: Slice in half; steam for 15 minutes.
Microwave: 7 minutes at 80% power.
Precook: 10 minutes in broth.
Pan-fry: Thinly-sliced, fry for 8 minutes (4 on each side).

Miso

Miso, a fermented soybean and grain paste, is a Japanese kitchen staple adapted from Chinese cuisine. It is often used in soups, gravies and sauces, in stir-frying, as a marinade, a pickling medium, as a stock and in salad dressings. In Western cuisine it can take the place of nut butters, tapenade or even pesto.

Traditionally, miso is created when bacterial culture (koji) is added to cooked soybeans. There are several types of miso—barley, rice and soybean—the difference among them being the base in which the koji was cultivated. The koji is cultivated separately in either a barley, rice or soybean base before being added to cooked soybeans. Varying the amount of soybeans, koji and salt results in misos ranging from dark to light and from sweet to salty in taste. Just like wine, each miso has its own distinctive flavour, colour and aroma. In *New Vegetarian Basics* I've used some basic and widely available misos in the recipes: rice, barley, chickpea and white (sweet or mellow) miso.

Misos with a higher salt and koji content and proportionately more soybeans are usually darker and saltier in taste. This type of miso is often marketed as barley, brown rice or chickpea miso. It must be fermented for a long period, often up to three years. White miso is high in rice and koji content, but low in salt and it ferments quickly, usually in eight weeks.

It is important to remember that miso contains abundant healthful bacteria that are easily destroyed by prolonged cooking. Never boil miso—it destroys the flavour and bacteria. Instead, add miso to your food just before it is removed from the heat. Miso can be stored in the refrigerator for up to six months.

Miso uses salt during the fermentation process and so is best avoided by people on a salt-free diet. For this reason, miso may also be used in place of salt or soy sauce in most recipes: ½ tsp (2 mL) salt = 1 tbsp (15 mL) barley miso or 1½ tbsp (22 mL) of white miso.

BEANS

Beans are available dried and canned. When buying dried whole beans, look for beans that are not gnarled, soft or cracked. Store dried beans at room temperature in a covered container. Canned beans may contain sugar, too much salt and additives, so read your labels carefully. To cook dried beans, follow the chart and steps below. Note that lentils and split peas do not need to be soaked before being cooked. Also, lentils range in size and will require different cooking times. Cooked beans can be stored in the fridge for one week or frozen for six months. Freeze beans in small 1- or 2-cup (250 or 500 mL) amounts. Or fill an old-fashioned ice-cube tray three-quarters full of cooked beans, add 2 tbsp (25 mL) water to each cube section and freeze for 24 hours. Remove frozen bean cubes from tray and place in a plastic bag. Then throw away the ice pick!

How to Cook Beans
1. Sort beans. Discard any stones, foreign matter or any discoloured beans or peas.
2. Rinse in cold water.
3. Cover beans with three to four times (see chart) their volume of water. Bring to a boil; remove from heat.
4. Soak for 6 hours (skip the soaking for lentils and split peas but do rinse them).
5. Discard soaking water. Rinse and add fresh water. Bring to a boil. Lower heat and simmer, partially covered (see chart for cooking times).
6. Add water as needed to keep beans covered. Do not add salt or other seasonings until beans are tender.

Dry Measure 1 cup (250 mL)	Water	Cooking Time	Yield
Adzuki	3 cups (750 mL)	45 minutes	3 cups (750 mL)
Black	3 cups (750 mL)	1½ hours	3 cups (500 mL)
Chickpeas	4 cups (1 L)	3 hours	2½ cups (625 mL)
Great Northern	3½ cups (875 mL)	2 hours	2½ cups (625 mL)
Kidney	3 cups (750 mL)	2 hours	2 cups (500 mL)
Lentils	3 cups (750 mL)	35–45 minutes	2¼ cups (550 mL)
Navy	3 cups (750 mL)	2½ hours	2 cups (500 mL)
Pinto	3 cups (750 mL)	2 hours	2 cups (500 mL)
Soybeans	4 cups (1 L)	3½ hours	3 cups (500 mL)
Split peas	3 cups (750 mL)	45 minutes	2½ cups (625 mL)

How to Avoid Gas

Beans have a reputation for producing gas in humans. This is because there are certain carbohydrates in beans that we cannot digest. These carbohydrates include complex sugars (raffinose in particular) that pass undigested into our lower intestine. There they encounter bacteria that causes them to ferment and thus cause gas. Blame it on fermented sugar! Soaking and cooking beans helps to release a large portion of raffinose so that when we eat them there will be less raffinose "presence" in our intestinal tract. Reduce the water-soluble villain and there's less fermentation and no carbon dioxide and hydrogen gases.

GRAINS AND RICE

The texture and nutty taste of grains and rice always add a delicious dynamic to vegetarian dishes. Typically, in diets of the world's traditional cultures, grains are eaten together with beans. This makes profound nutritional sense as beans contain the amino acids that are often deficient in grains. Today a range of "new but old" grains are springing into a grocery store near you. Grains such as quinoa or amaranth, ancient grains grown in agrarian societies centuries ago, are making huge comebacks as we discover their unique tastes and extraordinary nutritional profiles. Adding them to a vegetarian diet will expand your repertoire and ensure variety in taste and texture in your meals.

Generally, I prefer to use the whole grain rather than refined versions. Whole grains consist of four layers: The hull, the protective outer coating; the bran, a good source of fibre and the B vitamins; the germ, also a rich source of vitamins, particularly vitamin E, minerals, protein and oils; and finally the endosperm, the interior, starchy kernel. When grains are refined often the only layer retained in the processing is the endosperm. This means that the layers with the most nutritional benefit are removed.

The best way to cook grains and rice is to simmer them slowly in liquid, either water or stock. You can influence the flavour of the cooked grain depending on the choice of cooking stock. I prefer to use a basic vegetable stock as it intensifies the flavour of the grain and brings out its natural robust texture and taste.

Dry Measure 1 cup (250 mL)	Water or Stock	Cooking Time	Yield
Amaranth	2½ cups (625 mL)	25 minutes	2 cups (500 mL)
Arborio rice	6 cups (1.5 L)	20 minutes	4 cups (1 L)
Barley (hulled)	3 cups (750 mL)	1½ hours	3½ cups (875 mL)
Barley (pearl)	3 cups (750 mL)	50 minutes	3½ cups (875 mL)
Basmati rice (brown)	2¼ cups (550 mL)	45 minutes	3 cups (750 mL)
Basmati rice (white)	1¾ cups (425 mL)	15 minutes	3 cups (750 mL)
Brown rice	2 cups (500 mL)	45 minutes	3 cups (750 mL)
Buckwheat	2 cups (500 mL)	15 minutes	2½ cups (625 mL)
Bulgur wheat	1½ cups (375 mL)	20 minutes	2½ cups (625 mL)
Millet	3 cups (750 mL)	45 minutes	3½ cups (875 mL)
Quinoa	2 cups (500 mL)	15 minutes	2½ cups (625 mL)
Sushi rice	2 cups (500 mL)	20 minutes	2½ cups (625 mL)
Teff	1 cup (250 mL)	8 minutes	2 cups (500 mL)
Wild rice	3 cups (750 mL)	1 hour	4 cups (1 L)

How to Store Grains
Whole grains with their germ intact contain oils that will go rancid if not kept cool. Place grains in a freezer bag, label, date and refrigerate for up to four months.

How to Cook Grains
There are two ways to cook grains. Choose either the boiling water method or the cold water method (you can substitute stock or broth for water in both cases). In the boiling method, bring a pot of liquid to a boil, slowly add the rinsed grain, cover and reduce heat to simmer. In the cold water method, place rinsed grain in pot, add cold liquid, bring to a boil, cover, reduce heat and simmer.

Other tips to keep in mind:
- Use heavy pot with a lid.
- Measure grains in dry-ingredient measure.
- If all liquid has been absorbed but grains are not yet thoroughly cooked, stir in a few tablespoonfuls (15 mL) of boiling liquid, cover and cook over low heat.

How to Dry-Roast Grains

Dry-roasting grains changes the texture and to some degree the taste of a grain. A dry-roasted grain absorbs less water during cooking and makes the cooked grain chewier and less mushy. When roasting more than one type of grain, use separate skillets. Grains roast for different lengths of time.
- Measure grain, wash and drain in fine-mesh strainer.
- Heat heavy-bottomed skillet over medium-high heat until hot.
- Add grain and using wooden spoon, move grain around pan, turning each grain.
- When moisture has evaporated, reduce heat to medium-low and quickly stir grains until they begin to pop. Remove from heat and stir.

SEA VEGETABLES

Sea vegetables are under-used, nutritional powerhouse ingredients. Their delicate flavour and calcium-rich properties should make them an important part of a vegetarian diet. With today's increasing concern about over-population and food shortages arising from overworked and undernourished land, it is reassuring to know of the bountiful harvest lying hidden under coastlines, near and far.

There are 18,000 varieties of algae and most are marine. Marine algae are what we commonly call sea vegetables, seaweeds or sea greens. All three of these terms are inaccurate to some degree. Marine algae are certainly not weeds and most of those we use are brown or red. Sea vegetable is also misleading, for algae exhibit unique traits that are not at all shared by vegetables.

There are four basic types of algae: red, brown, green and blue-green. They are among the most ancient life-forms on earth. They have remained primitive due to the relatively small amount of change in their ocean environment. Ocean temperatures change more slowly and vary much less than land temperatures, because they depend on the temperature of the core of the earth, not that of the air. Compared to land plants, ocean plants do not experience severe changes. In many ways, sea vegetables are like photo-negatives of land plants. Marine algae are in constant motion, flexibly swaying with the rhythms of the sea while land plants have stiff, rooted structures with little movement except in strong winds.

Here are five of the most commonly available packaged sea plants to explore: agar-agar, arame, hijiki, kombu and nori (see also Glossary). They can be purchased in all Asian food stores and in most natural or health food stores. They are sold in sealed packages or in bulk in the dry form. They should be stored in a dry dark place. If plants pick up moisture during storage, place them in an oven at a low temperature until crispness is restored. Sea vegetables can be stored for up to a year.

Agar-agar
This sea vegetable has terrific jelling properties and can be added directly to simmering liquid. It's often combined with kudzu for jelling purposes

Arame
Soak arame in room-temperature water for 5 minutes before cooking.

Hijiki
Hijiki quadruples in volume so you need to be careful when measuring. It also needs to soak in cold water for 10 minutes. If you are adding it to liquid that will be cooked, such as soup, soak it for only 5 minutes and then add to your cooking liquid for the remaining 5 minutes.

Kombu
Kombu is sold dried in flat sheets or in strips measuring 6 to 8 inches (15 to 20 cm). It may have a white powdery water-soluble coating that contains lots of flavour so do not rinse kombu before cooking. It's also available powdered.

Nori
These thin sheets of seaweed can be bought toasted or untoasted but I prefer to use them toasted because the flavour is accentuated. To toast nori yourself, carefully pass each sheet for 10 seconds on each side over a flame or element. The colour of the nori will change from purple-brown to greenish-black.

NUTS AND SEEDS

Seeds and nuts are available raw, roasted, salted, unsalted, chopped or in the shell. They are best used in small amounts to enhance the nutrition and flavour of other ingredients in a meal. Because they are high in oils, they can be ground into butters or thick pastes and are a concentrated caloric source of protein.

When purchasing nuts and seeds, buy whole nuts. The actual meat of the nut should be whole, not in pieces. If it is broken, perishable oils are exposed to air and oxidation occurs, which produces rancidity. Discard nuts that contain dark areas, black spots or mould. When possible, buy refrigerated, organically grown nuts. Store them in the fridge to reduce rancidity for up to four months.

Toasting or Roasting Nuts and Seeds

Nuts and seeds can be toasted in a heavy (no liquid) skillet over medium-high heat, stirring several times to expose all sides. They release an aroma and turn darker, and seeds also pop and crackle. If you want to add tamari flavour to nuts and seeds, fill an all-purpose spray bottle with tamari, wait until the nuts and seeds begin to brown, about 3 minutes, then spray a coat of tamari that covers them, not the pan.

Some people use toaster ovens set at 350°F (180°C), stirring twice. Always pay close attention and use your nose to determine when they are ready. Most nuts require 5 minutes of roasting, seeds, 5 to 6 minutes.

FLAVOURINGS

The basic ingredients of beans, grains, sea vegetables or soy foods are the foundations of fabulous vegetarian cooking. But it's the additions of herbs, spices, vinegars and oils that really makes it sing. Be sure to buy top-quality, preferably organically grown, ingredients to add the freshest of tastes to your meals.

Herbs and Spices

Nothing increases flavour like fresh or dried herbs and spices. Herbs are leaves, stems and flowers of soft plants that are edible and flavourful. As a guide for interchanging fresh and dried herbs, ½ tsp (2 mL) dry = 1 tbsp (15 mL) fresh. Buy herbs in small amounts to store in airtight containers away from heat and light. Grind your own mixtures using a mortar and pestle. Spices are dried and often ground sections of buds, flowers, fruit, seeds, bark and roots of certain plants. Whole spices have a shelf life of six months so again it's best to buy them in small amounts. Grind whole spices in a coffee grinder or pepper mill.

Vinegars

Vinegar is an important ingredient in salad dressings but it can also enhance the taste of stews and soups. Vinegars are made by diluting the acid derived from fermented grains or fruit with water and range from acidic to sweet, depending how they are made. Acidity is often listed as a percentage on the label. A high-acidity vinegar has a 7 per cent level while a low-acidity vinegar has about 4 per cent. Low-acid vinegars require less oil to be added to them when making dressings—perfect for those low-fat dressings! When it comes to marinating beans and grains, it's best to use a vinegar with higher acidity. I like to use low-acid vinegar, such as balsamic, rice wine or fruit vinegars, to complement the flavour of salad greens.

Oils

Oils are extracted from grains, seeds, fruits and nuts. How they are extracted and to what degree of heat they were exposed is of concern. Read the labels! The oils I prefer have been extracted mechanically in an expeller press, and not exposed to high heat, hexane sovents, bleaching or deodorizing. These oils need to be refrigerated upon opening because they can become rancid upon extended exposure to air and light. Date the bottle and check it at six months.

I use several types of oils for varying purposes. For salad dressings, I prefer Italian extra virgin olive oil. When I want a flavour-free oil for sautéeing, I choose expeller-pressed canola oil. For stir-fries with ingredients that have an Asian twist—tofu or tempeh, ginger and soy sauce—I like to use toasted sesame oil. Its fragrance enhances the taste. See the Natural Foods Pantry on page 18 for a list of oils to have on hand.

THE NATURAL FOODS
PANTRY

What Is a Natural Food?

For me, whether a food is natural is determined not by what it contains, but by what it doesn't contain, things such as refined white sugar and flour, chemical preservatives and artificial flavours. The basic consideration is the origin of the ingredient: Is this food sold as fresh as possible with the least amount of processing or refining? The foods I term as "natural" have been minimally processed or the processing uses no chemicals, and there are no artificial ingredients added.

The Organic Question

Stores are now beginning to label their produce according to their growing methods. This allows consumers to make produce choices based on taste, pocketbook and availability. The three labels that you'll encounter most are:
1) conventionally grown;
2) transitionally grown;
3) organically grown.

Conventionally grown produce is grown with the use of chemical fertilizers and pesticides.

Transitionally grown produce is grown without the use of chemical fertilizers and pesticides but has not been grown in soil that has been certified organic. It takes three years of chemical-free application to qualify for organic certification.

Organically grown produce is certified to have been grown in soil that has been free of chemical fertilizers or pesticides for three years. Farmers use crop rotation to keep the soil fertile and spread composted organic material (leaves, leftover crops, manure) on their fields.

Organic fruits and vegetables are not perfect. We need to allow the organic movement its own "growing pains" as it continues to improve its growing, harvesting and shipping methods that will in turn enhance the product's appearance and shelf life. My preference is to buy organic, but even if you do I always advise that you wash *all* produce. Use a vegetable brush to remove surface dirt from vegetables with tough exteriors. Peel conventionally grown fruits and vegetables. Eliminate surface pesticide residue by washing in warm water. There are now "vegetable washes" available just for this purpose.

Organizing the Pantry

One of the most useful things I feel a cookbook can do for the busy or tired cook is to preplan or think through meal preparation. The following lists contain the ingredients you'll need to cook the recipes in this book and then some. Take them with you as a guide when food shopping. I borrow from a wide range of cuisines, including Thai, Indian, Mexican, Italian, French and Chinese. Check the Glossary for additional information about an unfamiliar ingredient. Many ingredients are easily substituted and I have noted the substitutions within the recipes.

Fresh Fruit
apples
apricots
bananas
berries (blueberry, raspberry, strawberry)
cherries
cranberries
dates
figs
lemons
limes
mangoes
melons (cantaloupe, honeydew, watermelon)
oranges
papayas
peaches
pears
pineapples
plums

Fresh Produce
asparagus
avocados
beets and beet greens
cabbage
celeriac (celery root)
celery
corn
eggplant (Mediterranean and Japanese)
English cucumber
fennel
garlic
green onions
kale
leeks
lemongrass
lettuce (Bibb, red leaf, romaine)
mushrooms (button, portobello, shiitake)
onions (Vidalia)
parsnips
peas
potatoes
spinach
sprouts (alfalfa, red clover)
squash (acorn, butternut)
sweet peppers (green and red)
sweet potatoes
Swiss chard

tomatoes
yams
zucchini

Dairy and Soy
butter
Cheddar cheese
eggs
goat cheese
low-fat yogurt (soy
    or dairy)
miso
Monterey Jack cheese
Parmesan cheese (soy
    or dairy)
rice milk
soy milk
tempeh
tofu
2% milk

Beans
adzuki
black
chickpeas (garbanzo)
Great Northern
kidney
lentils
navy
pinto
soybeans
split peas

Grains and Rice
amaranth
Arborio rice
barley (hulled and pearl)
basmati rice (brown
    and white)

brown rice
buckwheat
bulgur
millet
quinoa
sushi rice
teff
wheat germ
wild rice

Sea Vegetables
agar-agar
arame
hijiki
kombu
kudzu (*see* agar-agar)
nori

Flours
cornmeal
spelt
triticale
unbleached white flour
whole wheat flour (hard)
whole wheat flour (soft
    or pastry)

Nuts
almonds
cashews
chestnuts
coconut
filberts (hazelnut)
peanuts
pecans
pine nuts
pistachios
soynuts
walnuts

Seeds
alfalfa
flax
popping corn
poppy
pumpkin
sesame (black and beige)
sunflower

Nut and Seed Butters
almond (smooth and
    crunchy)
cashew
peanut (smooth and
    crunchy)
sesame (tahini)
soy
sunflower

Dried Fruits
apricots
cherries
cranberries
currants
dates
figs
prunes
raisins

Dry Goods
arrowroot flour
baking powder
baking soda
bread crumbs
coffee
dried mushrooms
fusilli pasta
good-tasting nutritional
    yeast

sea salt
soba noodles
sun-dried tomatoes
tea
tortilla chips
vegetable bouillon cubes

Canned Goods
artichoke hearts
black beans
capers
chickpeas
chilies
coconut milk
corn
crushed pineapple
kidney beans
olives (black and green)
pinto beans
pumpkin purée
salsa
tomato juice
tomato paste
tomato sauce
tomatoes (ground)

Freezer Goods
cooked beans
flax seeds
fruit
phyllo pastry
pie dough
pita bread
pizza dough
tortillas
vegetables (plain)

Oils
canola
extra virgin olive oil
flaxseed oil
toasted sesame oil

Vinegars
apple cider
balsamic
rice
umeboshi plum
wine vinegar

Herbs, Spices and Flavourings
allspice
anise
basil
bay leaf
caraway seed
cardamom
cayenne pepper
celery seed
chilies
chives
cilantro (coriander)
cinnamon
cloves
coriander (cilantro)
cumin
curry pastes
curry powder
dill
fennel
gingerroot
marjoram

mint
mustard seed
nutmeg
oregano
paprika
parsley
pepper (black)
rosemary
sage
tarragon
thyme
turmeric
vanilla

Sweeteners
brown rice syrup
brown sugar
maple syrup
molasses
Sucanat

Condiments
chutney
curry paste
Dijon mustard
hot pepper sauce
ketchup
mirin
pickled ginger
pickled peppers
pickles
soy mayonnaise
soy sauce
tamari
umeboshi plum paste
wasabi

1
Appetizers and Snacks

■ ■ ■

Mushroom Pepper Bruschetta

Stuffed Nori Trumpets

Spinach Sushi

Navy Bean Pâté

Nachos

Vegetable Latkes

Vegetarian Chopped Liver

Breaded Tofu with Almonds

Tofu Neatballs

Grilled Portobello Mushrooms with Bulgur Salad

Baked Pink Popcorn

Pita Pizzas

Baked Artichoke Dip

Roasted Pepper and Chickpea Dip

Tempeh and Chickpea Spread

Split Pea Tofu Spread

Tofu Olive Spread

Shiitake Mushroom and Roasted Tamari Almond Dip

Basil and Sun-Dried Tomato Dip

Wasabi Spread

Tangy Tofu Spread

Mango Kiwi Salsa

Mushroom Pepper Bruschetta

———

This fragrant appetizer is a guaranteed crowd-pleaser that must be eaten right away.

Preparation time: 25 minutes

Preheat broiler

Cooking time: 2 minutes

Makes 12 pieces

2 tbsp	olive oil	25 mL
1	each sweet red and yellow pepper, chopped	1
3	green onions, thinly sliced	3
3	cloves garlic, minced	3
2 cups	chopped mixed mushrooms (portobello, shiitake or button)	500 mL
2 tbsp	chopped fresh basil	25 mL
½ tsp	dried thyme	2 mL
¼ cup	freshly grated Parmesan cheese	50 mL
1 tsp	balsamic vinegar	5 mL
¼ tsp	each salt and freshly ground black pepper	1 mL
12	slices (1 inch/2.5 cm thick) baguette	12
½ cup	grated Asiago cheese	125 mL

In large skillet, heat oil over medium heat. Cook red and yellow peppers, onions and garlic for 3 minutes. Add mushrooms; cover and cook for 5 minutes or until softened.

Add basil and thyme; cook, uncovered and stirring, for 5 minutes. Remove from heat. Stir in Parmesan, vinegar, salt and pepper.

Spoon 2 tbsp (25 mL) mushroom mixture onto each bread slice; sprinkle with 2 tsp (10 mL) Asiago. Place on baking sheet. Broil for 2 minutes or until cheese has melted. Serve immediately.

Per piece: 106 calories · 4 g protein · 5 g total fat · 12 g carbohydrate · 1 g fibre · 2 g saturated fat · 6 mg cholesterol · 223 mg sodium · excellent source vitamin C

Stuffed Nori Trumpets

My family and I were reading about the fall of Jericho when Joshua blew a shofar (ram horn) and the walls came tumbling down. The kids remembered some stuffed nori cones I once made and wanted to know if they could cause walls to fall too! This recipe evolved out of a spring cleaning when I wanted to use up ingredients that were "on the verge." It's an appetizing alternative to sushi.

Preparation time: 1 hour

Makes 24 pieces

1 cup	wild rice, washed	250 mL
1 cup	brown rice, washed	250 mL
1 tbsp	wasabi powder	15 mL
½ cup	tamari	125 mL
¼ cup	mirin	50 mL
¼ cup	rice vinegar	50 mL
2 tbsp	water	25 mL
1-¼ cups	sprouts	300 mL
1 cup	grated carrot	250 mL
¾ cup	toasted pumpkin seeds	175 mL
3	green onions, sliced in ¼-inch (5 mm) rings	3
6	sheets nori, toasted	6

In saucepan, bring 4½ cups (1.125 L) water to boil. Stir in wild and brown rice; cover, reduce heat and simmer for 50 minutes or until just tender. Transfer to large bowl; set aside to cool.

Mix wasabi powder with 1 tsp (5 mL) water; combine with tamari, mirin, rice vinegar and water. Pour over cooling rice and mix gently. Let cool completely.

Set ¼ cup (50 mL) of the sprouts aside for garnish. Add remaining sprouts to bowl along with carrot, pumpkin seeds and green onions; mix gently until combined.

With scissors, cut nori sheets into quarters. On each quarter, place large tablespoonful (15 mL) filling in centre; wrap nori around filling in cone shape. Seal overlapping sides with a few drops of water. Garnish each cone with reserved sprouts.

Per piece: 102 calories · 5 g protein · 3 g total fat · 13 g carbohydrate · 2 g fibre (moderate) · 1 g saturated fat · 0 mg cholesterol · 344 mg sodium

Spinach Sushi

═══ ═══ ═══

This is the perfect party food. I have taught more people to roll sushi socially than in a classroom. I always have the ingredients ready to roll, add the rice, mustard paste and spinach, then using my trusted rolling mat, assemble a truly delicious appetizer. I say it's all in the wrist.

Preparation time: 40 minutes

Makes 12 pieces

½ cup	sushi rice	125 mL
1 tbsp	mirin	15 mL
2 tsp	rice vinegar	10 mL
Pinch	salt	Pinch
2 tbsp	each brown and black sesame seeds	25 mL
2	pkg (each 10 oz/300 g) spinach, stemmed and washed	2
2 tsp	soy sauce	10 mL
2 tsp	Dijon mustard	10 mL
½ tsp	wasabi powder	2 mL
½ tsp	water	2 mL
2	sheets nori, toasted	2
DIPPING SAUCE:		
2 tbsp	soy sauce	25 mL
1 tsp	wasabi powder	5 mL
¼ cup	water	50 mL

In sieve, rinse rice well until water runs clear. In medium saucepan, bring 1 cup (250 mL) water to boil. Add rice, mirin, rice vinegar and salt; return to boil. Cover, reduce heat and simmer for 15 minutes or until liquid has been absorbed. Do not stir. Keep warm.

Meanwhile, in dry skillet over medium heat, toast sesame seeds until they pop, about 5 minutes. Place in shallow bowl.

In large pot of boiling water, cook spinach just until wilted, about 2 minutes. Drain and refresh in bowl of ice water; drain and squeeze out excess water. Chop very finely. Sprinkle with soy sauce. Shape into 2 equal logs. Roll logs in sesame seeds to coat well. Set aside.

In small bowl, mix together mustard, wasabi and water to make paste. Set aside.

Place 1 nori sheet on sushi mat with short end facing you. Spoon ½ cup (125 mL) warm rice onto sheet. Press rice firmly with spatula to cover sheet, leaving 1-inch (2.5 cm) border at top and bottom. Spread half of the mustard paste over rice.

Place spinach log widthwise across sheet on bottom third. To roll, lift sushi mat at edge closest to you and begin to roll up, holding filling in place with index fingers. Roll up nori firmly, like jelly roll, almost to end. Using finger tip, moisten top strip of uncovered nori with some water to seal roll. Cut each roll into 6 pieces with serrated knife. Fill, roll and cut remaining nori.

Dipping Sauce: In small bowl, mix together soy sauce, wasabi powder and water. Serve with sushi.

Per piece: 61 calories · 3 g protein · 2 g total fat · 9 g carbohydrate · 1 g fibre · trace saturated fat · 0 mg cholesterol · 276 mg sodium · excellent source folacin

Navy Bean Pâté

━━ ━━ ━━

Delicious on crackers or bread, this also is the makings of tasty sandwiches.

Preparation time: 15 minutes

Chilling time: 30 minutes

Makes 2 cups (500 mL)

1	slice whole grain bread, crusts removed	1
1	can (14 oz/398 mL) navy beans, drained and rinsed	1
¼ cup	chopped pistachios	50 mL
¼ cup	fresh lemon juice	50 mL
1 tbsp	extra virgin olive oil	15 mL
1 tbsp	chopped fresh dill	15 mL
1 tbsp	minced capers	15 mL
2	cloves garlic, minced	2
¼ tsp	salt	1 mL
Pinch	cayenne pepper	Pinch

Tear bread into pieces; sprinkle with 1 tbsp (15 mL) water and set aside to soak.

In food processor fitted with metal blade, process beans, pistachios, lemon juice, oil, dill, capers, garlic, salt and cayenne until smooth. Add bread and purée.

Transfer to airtight container; refrigerate until chilled. (Pâté can be refrigerated for up to 2 days.)

Per tbsp (15 mL): 24 calories · 1 g protein · 1 g total fat · 3 g carbohydrate · 1 g fibre · 0 g saturated fat · 0 mg cholesterol · 66 mg sodium

Nachos

━━ ━━ ━━

Quick, satisfying and certainly the easiest recipe in the book, these nachos will be a hit.

Preparation time: 5 minutes

Preheat oven to 400°F (200°C)

Cooking time: 5 minutes

Makes 6 servings

1	pkg (9 oz/255 g) salted corn chips	1
1 cup	salsa	250 mL
1 cup	cooked pinto beans	250 mL
1-½ cups	grated old Cheddar or Monterey Jack cheese	375 mL
2	green onions, chopped	2

Lay out chips in single layer on 11- x 17-inch (45 x 29 cm) rimmed baking sheet. Spread salsa evenly over chips, followed by beans. Cover with grated cheese. Sprinkle with onions. Bake in 400°F (200°C) oven for 5 to 7 minutes or until cheese is bubbly.

Per serving: 377 calories · 13 g protein · 21 g total fat · 37 g carbohydrate · 6 g fibre (very high)
· 8 g saturated fat · 30 mg cholesterol · 514 mg sodium
· excellent source calcium, folacin

Vegetable Latkes

— ▭ ▭ ▭ —

These are not ordinary latkes. The potatoes are boiled, mashed with other vegetables and then fried in a little oil. Everyone loves them. Serve with apple sauce or Tofu Sour Cream (page 87). Latkes can be cooked ahead and reheated on parchment paper-lined baking sheet in 400°F (200°C) oven until warmed through, about 8 minutes.

Preparation time: 35 minutes
Makes 12 latkes

1 lb	potatoes, scrubbed and quartered	500 g
1	sweet potato, scrubbed and quartered	1
1	large carrot, sliced	1
1	large onion, halved	1
4	cloves garlic	4
2 tbsp	chopped fresh parsley	25 mL
1 tsp	salt	5 mL
½ tsp	freshly ground black pepper	2 mL
½ cup	each bread crumbs and good-tasting nutritional yeast	125 mL
1 tbsp	paprika	15 mL
2 tbsp	olive oil	25 mL

Place potatoes, carrot, onion and garlic in large pot; cover with 8 cups (2 L) water. Bring to boil; reduce heat and simmer for 15 minutes or until vegetables are softened. Drain, reserving ¼ cup (50 mL) water.

Mash vegetables until somewhat coarse. Stir in reserved cooking water, parsley, salt and pepper. Using ¼ cup (50 mL) measure, form into twelve ¼-inch (5 mm) thick patties.

In shallow dish, combine bread crumbs, good-tasting nutritional yeast and paprika. Coat latkes with crumb mixture.

In large skillet, heat oil over medium heat. Cook latkes, in batches and turning once, for 10 minutes or until browned.

Per latke: 130 calories · 4 g protein · 4 g total fat · 22 g carbohydrate · 2 g fibre (moderate) · trace saturated fat · 0 mg cholesterol · 237 mg sodium · excellent source folacin

---

New Vegetarian Basics

Vegetarian Chopped Liver

My Aunt Jenny has been making her own chopped liver for 70 years. She is a true expert, so I knew what I was up against. For her 85th birthday party, I tried my hand and made this recipe. Then, with a few crackers and rice cakes, the taste test began. "Nettie," she said with approval, "I can taste the pistachios." This also makes a great sandwich filling.

Preparation time: 20 minutes

Chilling time: 1 hour

Makes 3 cups (750 mL)

2 tbsp	olive oil	25 mL
3	onions, diced	3
¼ tsp	dried rosemary	1 mL
1 tbsp	mirin	15 mL
2 cups	green beans	500 mL
2	hard-boiled eggs	2
1 cup	toasted pistachios	250 mL
2 tbsp	sun-dried tomato purée or tomato paste	25 mL
1 tbsp	mayonnaise or tofu mayonnaise	15 mL
1 tsp	salt	5 mL
Pinch	freshly ground black pepper	Pinch

In skillet, heat oil over medium heat. Cook onions with rosemary for 5 minutes or until softened. Add mirin; cook for 5 minutes.

Steam beans until soft, about 6 minutes; transfer to food processor. Add onions, eggs and pistachios; purée until well blended, scraping down sides.

Add tomato purée, mayonnaise, salt and pepper; process until very smooth. Chill for at least 1 hour.

Per tbsp (15 mL): 31 calories · 1 g protein · 2 g total fat · 2 g carbohydrate · 1 g fibre · trace saturated fat · 9 mg cholesterol · 53 mg sodium

Breaded Tofu with Almonds

Once for a cooking demonstration I had to deep-fry tofu and smother it in good-tasting nutritional yeast (see Glossary). It was tough extolling the yeast's flavour when the tofu was really a soggy mess. So I vowed to create a recipe that would enhance its flavour. Even my skeptical recipe tester, Kate Gammal, had to admit that this tasted very good. Can be served as an appetizer or as a side dish.

Preparation time: 15 minutes
Makes 2 servings

2	eggs, beaten	2
⅓ cup	good-tasting nutritional yeast	75 mL
8 oz	firm tofu, rinsed, pressed and sliced into 1 x 1½ x ¼-inch (2.5 x 4 cm x 5mm)	250 g
2 tbsp	olive oil	25 mL
3	green onions, chopped	3
¼ cup	chopped fresh coriander	50 mL
¼ cup	sliced almonds	50 mL
1 tbsp	fresh lemon juice	15 mL

Place eggs in shallow bowl. In another shallow bowl, place yeast. Coat tofu pieces in egg, then in yeast; place on plate.

In nonstick skillet, heat oil over medium heat. Cook tofu, turning once, for 6 minutes or until browned.

Stir in green onions, coriander, almonds and lemon juice.

Per appetizer serving: 201 calories · 13 g protein · 18 g total fat · 4 g carbohydrate · 1 g fibre · 2 g saturated fat · 108 mg cholesterol · 41 mg sodium · excellent source folacin

---

New Vegetarian Basics

Tofu Neatballs

My son, Cameron, became very curious about the variety of foods he saw at a potluck party we attended together. When he asked why we couldn't eat meatballs I decided to make up this version of the traditional meatball using frozen tofu (page 6)—Cameron loved it!

Serve these with pasta or tucked into a pita.

Preparation time: 20 minutes
Makes 24 balls

1 lb	frozen tofu, thawed, squeezed dry and crumbled	500 g
2 tbsp	soy sauce	25 mL
1 tsp	mirin	5 mL
3	cloves garlic, minced	3
¾ cup	whole grain bread crumbs	175 mL
⅓ cup	freshly grated Parmesan cheese	75 mL
¼ cup	chopped fresh sage	50 mL
1 tsp	each dried oregano and basil	5 mL
2	eggs, lightly beaten	2
1	egg white	1
2 tbsp	olive oil	25 mL

In bowl, mix together tofu, soy sauce, mirin and garlic; let stand for 5 minutes. Stir in bread crumbs, cheese, sage, oregano, basil, eggs and egg white.

Shape heaping tablespoonfuls (15 mL) into tightly packed balls. In large skillet, heat oil over medium-high heat; brown balls on all sides, about 10 minutes.

Per ball: 43 calories · 3 g protein · 3 g total fat · 1 g carbohydrate · 0 g fibre · 1 g saturated fat · 19 mg cholesterol · 129 mg sodium

Grilled Portobello Mushrooms with Bulgur Salad

━━━ ━━━ ━━━

I adore portobello mushrooms. In this recipe they readily absorb the garlic and citrus flavours. Enjoy this as a light main course or as an inviting appetizer.

Preparation time: 30 minutes

Preheat grill to high

Cooking time: 8 minutes

Makes 4 servings

3 tbsp	olive oil	50 mL
1	clove garlic, minced	1
½ cup	fresh orange juice	125 mL
½ cup	dry white wine	125 mL
½ cup	bulgur	125 mL
2 tbsp	chopped fresh tarragon	25 mL
½ tsp	salt	2 mL
4	large portobello mushrooms, stemmed	4
¼ tsp	freshly ground black pepper	1 mL
2 tbsp	balsamic vinegar	25 mL
¼ cup	chopped fresh parsley	50 mL

In small saucepan, heat 1 tbsp (15 mL) of the oil over medium heat. Cook garlic for 3 minutes. Add all but 2 tbsp (25 mL) of the orange juice and wine; bring to boil. Reduce heat and simmer for 10 minutes or until reduced to ½ cup (125 mL). Keep warm.

In separate small saucepan, bring ¾ cup (175 mL) water to boil; stir in bulgur, tarragon and ¼ tsp (1 mL) of the salt. Cover and let stand for 10 minutes or until water is absorbed. Fluff with fork; cover and keep warm.

In small bowl, whisk together remaining oil and orange juice; brush on both sides of mushrooms. Sprinkle with remaining salt and pepper. Place mushrooms, top down, on grill over high heat; grill, covered and turning once, for 8 minutes or until softened. Drizzle with vinegar.

Place each mushroom, top down, on plate. Top each with about ½ cup (125 mL) bulgur; sprinkle with 1 tbsp (15 mL) parsley. Pour 2 tbsp (25 mL) reduced orange sauce over each.

Per serving: 201 calories · 4 g protein · 11 g total fat · 22 g carbohydrate · 4 g fibre (high) · 1 g saturated fat · 0 mg cholesterol · 295 mg sodium · good source iron, vitamin C, folacin

Baked Pink Popcorn

This sweet and tomatoey snack is so delicious that guests will keep coming back for more.

Preparation time: 5 minutes

Preheat oven to 200°F (100°C)

Cooking time: 1 hour

Makes 10 cups (2.5 L)

3 tbsp	liquid honey	50 mL
3 tbsp	tomato paste	50 mL
½ tsp	paprika	2 mL
¼ tsp	chili powder	1 mL
1	pkg (99 g) microwave popping corn, popped, or 1¼ cups (300 mL) popping corn, popped	1
⅓ cup	freshly grated Parmesan cheese	75 mL

In saucepan over medium heat, combine honey, tomato paste, paprika and chili powder, stirring, for 3 minutes. Place popped corn in large bowl; drizzle with honey mixture and toss to coat. Sprinkle with Parmesan and toss again.

Spread popcorn on ungreased 11- x 17-inch (29 x 45 cm) rimmed baking sheet. Bake in 200°F (100°C) oven for 15 minutes, stirring every 5 minutes. Turn oven off. Let dry in oven for 45 minutes.

Per cup (250 mL): 74 calories · 3 g protein · 2 g total fat · 13 g carbohydrate · 0 g fibre · 1 g saturated fat · 3 mg cholesterol · 66 mg sodium

Pita Pizzas

These pitas accommodate many types of toppings. For one children's birthday party, I sliced, grated and diced ingredients and had all the six-year-olds assemble their own lunches. Watching eight rowdy boys decorate their pitas was almost surreal. And they ate them too!

Preparation time: 15 minutes

Prehcat broiler

Cooking time: 5 minutes

Makes 4 servings

¼ cup	tomato sauce	50 mL
2	pita breads, split into 2 rounds	2
½ cup	grated mozzarella cheese	125 mL
Pinch	each dried or chopped fresh basil, oregano and thyme	Pinch
1	medium carrot, grated	1
1	medium sweet red pepper, thinly sliced	1
¼ cup	thinly sliced mushrooms	50 mL
1	medium tomato, sliced	1
¼ cup	olives, sliced	50 mL
1	small zucchini, sliced	1
Half	red onion, thinly sliced	Half
¼ cup	freshly grated Parmesan cheese	50 mL

Spread tomato sauce over pita rounds. Sprinkle with mozzarella.

Top with basil, oregano, thyme, carrot, red pepper, mushrooms, tomato, olives, zucchini and onion. Sprinkle with Parmesan.

Broil for 5 minutes or until cheese is bubbling.

Per serving: 216 calories · 10 g protein · 7 g total fat · 30 g carbohydrate · 3 g fibre (moderate) · 4 g saturated fat · 18 mg cholesterol · 452 mg sodium · excellent source vitamin C · good source calcium, folacin

Baked Artichoke Dip

═══ ═══ ═══

Make this delectable dip with artichokes canned in spring water, not oil. Smooth on slices of Russian rye bread or serve with chips or vegetables for dipping.

Preparation time: 10 minutes

Preheat oven to 375°F (190°C)

Cooking time: 20 minutes

Makes 2 cups (500 mL)

1	can (14 oz/398 mL) artichoke hearts, drained	1
4	large cloves garlic	4
½ cup	freshly grated Parmesan cheese	125 mL
¼ cup	each mayonnaise and cream cheese	50 mL
1 tbsp	fresh lemon juice	15 mL
½ cup	toasted pine nuts	125 mL

In food processor fitted with metal blade, finely chop artichoke hearts and garlic. Add all but 2 tbsp (25 mL) of the Parmesan, mayonnaise, cream cheese and lemon juice; process until smooth.

Evenly spread in 4-cup (1 L) ovenproof dish. Sprinkle with remaining cheese and pine nuts. Bake in 375°F (190°C) oven for 20 minutes or until bubbly.

Per tbsp (15 mL): 50 calories · 2 g protein · 4 g total fat · 2 g carbohydrate · 1 g fibre · 1 g saturated fat · 4 mg cholesterol · 52 mg sodium

New Vegetarian Basics

Roasted Pepper and Chickpea Dip

———

I love to serve this dip with slices of fresh crusty baguette.

Preparation time: 5 minutes
Makes 2 cups (500 mL)

1	clove garlic, minced	1
1 tbsp	olive oil	15 mL
1 tbsp	balsamic vinegar	15 mL
1 tbsp	mirin	15 mL
1	can (14 oz/398 mL) chickpeas, drained	1
2	roasted red peppers, peeled and seeded, reserving juice	2
1 tbsp	chopped fresh coriander	15 mL
½ tsp	salt	2 mL

In food processor, combine garlic, oil, vinegar, mirin, chickpeas, red peppers and reserved juices; purée until smooth. Stir in coriander and salt.

Tip: To roast peppers, slice in half and place peel side up on baking sheet. Bake in preheated 400°F (200°C) oven for about 20 minutes or until charred. Remove to bowl and cover with plastic wrap. Once cooled, peel and seed, reserving juices to add to dip.

Per tbsp (15 mL): 18 calories · 1 g protein · 1 g total fat · 3 g carbohydrate · trace fibre · 0 g saturated fat · 0 mg cholesterol · 55 mg sodium

Tempeh and Chickpea Spread

———

Here's a perfect protein hummus at last! This spread is made with soy tempeh which includes all eight essential amino acids.

Preparation time: 30 minutes

Makes 3 cups (750 mL)

4 oz	tempeh, sliced in 4 pieces	125 g
2	pieces (6 inch/15 cm each) kombu	2
1	can (19 oz/540 mL) chickpeas	1
¼ cup	tahini	50 mL
¼ cup	fresh lemon juice	50 mL
¼ tsp	each salt and ground cumin	1 mL
2	cloves garlic, minced	2
¼ cup	chopped fresh coriander	50 mL
2 tbsp	chopped chives	25 mL

In small saucepan, bring 1 cup (250 mL) water, tempeh and kombu to simmer; simmer for 20 minutes, turning tempeh occasionally. Discard kombu and water; let cool.

Meanwhile, drain chickpeas, reserving ¼ cup (50 mL) liquid. Rinse chickpeas; add to food processor along with reserved liquid and tahini; purée. Add lemon juice, salt, cumin and garlic; process until smooth.

Crumble tempeh into mixture. Add coriander and chives. Pulse just until blended, retaining texture of tempeh. (Spread can be refrigerated in airtight container for up to 3 days.)

Per tbsp (15 mL): 24 calories · 1 g protein · 1 g total fat · 3 g carbohydrate · trace fibre · 0 g saturated fat · 0 mg cholesterol · 34 mg sodium

Split Pea Tofu Spread

Stuff pieces of celery with this spread or enjoy it on crackers and crusty bread.

Preparation time: 10 minutes
Makes 1 cup (250 mL)

1 cup	cooked green split peas (see page 8 to 9)	250 mL
¼ cup	firm tofu, rinsed	50 mL
2 tbsp	mayonnaise	25 mL
2 tbsp	freshly grated Parmesan or Romano cheese	25 mL
¾ tsp	dried basil	4 mL
¼ tsp	each salt and freshly ground black pepper	1 mL

In food processor fitted with metal blade, pulse together peas, tofu, mayonnaise, cheese, basil, salt and pepper until smooth. (Spread can be refrigerated in airtight container for up to 5 days.)

Per tbsp (15 mL): 34 calories · 2 g protein · 2 g total fat · 3 g carbohydrate · trace fibre · trace saturated fat · 2 mg cholesterol · 60 mg sodium

Tofu Olive Spread

═ ═ ═

Surround this tangy dip with lots of cut up veggies and watch everyone come back for more. It's also perfect as a sandwich spread.

Preparation time: 10 minutes
Makes 1½ cups (375 mL)

8 oz	firm tofu, rinsed	250 g
2 tbsp	white miso	25 mL
2 tbsp	tahini	25 mL
2 tbsp	mayonnaise	25 mL
1 tbsp	apple cider vinegar	15 mL
1 tsp	dried dillweed	5 mL
8	calamata olives, pitted	8

In food processor fitted with metal blade, purée together tofu, miso, tahini and mayonnaise until smooth.

Add vinegar, dill and olives; purée until combined. (Spread can be refrigerated in airtight container for up to 5 days.)

Per tbsp (15 mL): 29 calories · 1 g protein · 2 g total fat · 1 g carbohydrate · trace fibre
· trace saturated fat · 1 mg cholesterol · 85 mg sodium

Shiitake Mushroom and Roasted Tamari Almond Dip

━━ ━━ ━━

Serve this unusual dip with vegetables, pita triangles or corn chips. Or try it spread on French bread. You can buy tamari-roasted almonds or roast them yourself (see page 13).

Preparation time: 45 minutes
Chilling time: 30 minutes
Makes 2 cups (500 mL)

18	dried shiitake mushrooms	18
2 tbsp	toasted sesame oil	25 mL
2	large onions, thinly sliced	2
½ tsp	dried thyme	2 mL
½ cup	tamari-roasted almonds, finely ground	125 mL
½ tsp	sea salt	2 mL

Place mushrooms in medium bowl. Pour in 3 cups (750 mL) boiling water to cover mushrooms by ½ inch (1 cm). Cover and set aside to soak for 20 minutes. Drain, reserving ½ cup (125 mL) liquid. Trim off tough stems and discard; quarter caps.

Meanwhile, in large skillet, heat oil over medium heat. Cook onions for 10 minutes or until softened and golden. Add mushrooms and 1 tbsp (15 mL) of the reserved soaking liquid; cook for 2 minutes. Add thyme.

Transfer to food processor. Add remaining soaking liquid; purée. Add almonds and salt; purée until smooth. Transfer to bowl; chill in refrigerator for 30 minutes.

Per tbsp (15 mL): 20 calories · trace protein · 1 g total fat · 2 g carbohydrate · trace fibre · 0 g saturated fat · 0 mg cholesterol · 32 mg sodium

Basil and Sun-Dried Tomato Dip

━━ ━━ ━━

Full of sunny Mediterranean flavour, this dip also makes an excellent sandwich spread.

Preparation time: 35 minutes

Chilling time: 30 minutes

Makes 2½ cups (625 mL)

1 lb	firm tofu, rinsed	500 g
½ cup	dry-packed sun-dried tomatoes, rehydrated	125 mL
½ cup	packed fresh basil leaves	125 mL
1 tbsp	olive oil	15 mL
2	cloves garlic, minced	2
¼ cup	toasted pistachios	50 mL
2 tbsp	balsamic vinegar	25 mL
½ tsp	salt	2 mL
Pinch	freshly ground black pepper	Pinch

Press tofu for 20 minutes (see pages 5 to 6).

To rehydrate tomatoes, bring tomatoes and ½ cup (125 mL) water to boil in small saucepan. Reduce heat and simmer gently for 10 minutes.

Transfer tomatoes and any remaining liquid to food processor along with basil, oil and garlic; process until smooth.

Add pressed tofu, pistachios, vinegar, salt and pepper; blend until smooth. Transfer to bowl; cover and chill in refrigerator for 30 minutes. (Dip can be refrigerated in airtight container for up to 5 days.)

Per tbsp (15 mL): 20 calories · 1 g protein · 1 g total fat · 1 g carbohydrate · 0 g fibre · 0 g saturated fat · 0 mg cholesterol · 47 mg sodium

Wasabi Spread

━ ━ ━

Smooth and creamy, this is a delectable sandwich spread.

Preparation time: 10 minutes

Makes 1 cup (250 mL)

4 oz	light cream cheese	125 g
4 oz	firm tofu, rinsed	125 g
1	clove garlic, minced	1
¼ cup	fresh coriander, coarsely chopped	50 mL
1 tbsp	chopped chives	15 mL
2 tsp	wasabi powder	10 mL

In food processor, blend together cream cheese, tofu, garlic, coriander, chives and wasabi powder until very smooth. (Spread can be refrigerated in airtight container for up to 5 days.)

Tip: Wasabi, often referred to as Japanese horseradish, is made from dried wasabi root. Sold in small tins or packets, it can be found in most health food stores or Asian supermarkets.

Per tbsp (15 mL): 25 calories · 1 g protein · 2 g total fat · 1 g carbohydrate · 0 g fibre · 1 g saturated fat · 7 mg cholesterol · 36 mg sodium

Tangy Tofu Spread

This piquant sandwich spread keeps well for up to three days in the refrigerator.

Preparation time: 10 minutes

Makes 2 cups (500 mL)

2 cups	firm tofu (approx 1 lb/500 g), rinsed	500 mL
½ cup	lemon juice	125 mL
½ cup	good-tasting nutritional yeast	125 mL
½ cup	tahini	125 mL
¼ cup	tamari	50 mL
¼ cup	chopped fresh basil	50 mL
2	cloves garlic, minced	2
1	pkg (10 oz/300 g) fresh spinach, washed, steamed and well drained	1

In food processor fitted with metal blade, process tofu, lemon juice, yeast, tahini, tamari, basil, garlic and spinach until smooth.

Per tbsp (15 mL): 22 calories · 2 g protein · 2 g total fat · 1 g carbohydrate · trace fibre · 0 g saturated fat · 0 mg cholesterol · 71 mg sodium

Mango Kiwi Salsa

Fresh fruit and chilies are a winning combination. This salsa goes well with Great Northern Bean Cakes (page 156) but can also be served as a relish with burgers or marinated tofu and tempeh.

Preparation time: 10 minutes
Chilling time: 6 hours
Makes 2½ cups (625 mL)

1 cup	diced peeled kiwifruit (about 3 kiwifruit)	250 mL
1	medium mango, peeled and diced	1
Half	serrano chili, seeded and minced	Half
1 cup	diced pineapple	250 mL
1 tbsp	fresh lime juice	15 mL
1 tbsp	chopped fresh coriander	15 mL
1 tsp	freshly grated gingerroot	5 mL
1 tsp	finely chopped fresh mint	5 mL

In glass bowl, mix together kiwifruit, mango, chili, pineapple, lime juice, coriander, ginger and mint. Chill for 6 hours to allow flavours to blend.

Per tbsp (15 mL): 9 calories · 0 g protein · 0 g total fat · 2 g carbohydrate · trace fibre · 0 g saturated fat · 0 mg cholesterol · 0 mg sodium

2
Soups

Vegetable Stock

Carrot Lentil Soup

Mushroom Veggie Broth

Sea Vegetable Chowder with Pesto

Aunt Jenny's Split Pea and Lentil Soup

Split Pea Soup

Cuban Black Bean Soup

Potato and Celery Soup with Celeriac

Cabbage Soup

Chickpea Miso Soup with Chilies and Lemongrass

Tofu Minestrone

Creamy Broccoli Soup

Miso Soup with Spinach and Sea Vegetables

Potato, Leek and Asparagus Soup

Curried Lentil Soup

Leek, Parsnip and Quinoa Soup

Mediterranean Vegetable Chowder

Dill and Chickpea Vegetable Broth

Sweet Potato Coconut Soup

Pumpkin Soup with Dried Cranberries

Vegetable Stock

▬ ▭ ▬

This recipe makes a lovely, clear broth full of flavour with a double pur-pose. Strain out the vegetables for an exceptional soup base. Or, leave in the vegetables for a terrific vegetable soup—I often eat it this way.

Preparation time: 1 hour

Makes 10 cups (2.5 L)

¼ cup	olive oil	50 mL
2	red onions, sliced	2
2	large leeks (white and light green parts only), rinsed and sliced	2
4	carrots, sliced	4
2 cups	mushrooms, halved	500 mL
2	stalks celery, sliced	2
1	sweet potato, peeled and cubed	1
10	sprigs parsley	10
10	peppercorns	10
4	sprigs fresh thyme	4
3	bay leaves	3

In large stockpot, heat oil over medium-high heat. Cook onions and leeks for 5 minutes or until softened. Add carrots, mushrooms, celery and potato; cook for 7 minutes.

Add parsley, peppercorns, thyme and bay leaves; cover with 10 cups (2.5 L) water and bring to boil. Reduce heat and simmer, covered, for 40 minutes.

Drain well through fine sieve, pressing with spoon to release liquid. Let cool. (Stock can be refrigerated in airtight container for up to 5 days or frozen.)

Per cup (250 mL): 50 calories · 0 g protein · 5 g total fat · 1 g carbohydrate · 0 g fibre · 1 g saturated fat · 0 mg cholesterol · 9 mg sodium

Carrot Lentil Soup

This is a version of the customer favourite served at the Big Carrot Natural Food Store in Toronto.

Preparation time: 30 minutes

Makes 6 servings

1 cup	dried lentils	250 mL
6 cups	vegetable stock (page 49) or water	1.5 L
3	large carrots, sliced	3
2 tbsp	olive oil	25 mL
1	onion, diced	1
3	cloves garlic, minced	3
1	sweet green pepper, chopped	1
½ cup	hijiki, soaked in 1 cup (250 mL) cold water for 5 minutes and drained	125 mL
1 tsp	each paprika and salt	5 mL
¼ tsp	freshly ground nutmeg	1 mL
¼ tsp	cayenne pepper	1 mL
2 tbsp	chopped fresh parsley	25 mL

Rinse lentils. In medium saucepan, bring lentils and stock to boil; reduce heat and simmer, covered, for 20 minutes until softened.

Meanwhile, steam carrots for 10 minutes or until tender, reserving ¼ cup (50 mL) cooking water. In food processor fitted with metal blade or in blender, purée together lentil mixture, carrots and reserved cooking water until smooth. Return to saucepan.

In skillet, heat oil over medium-high heat. Cook onion and garlic for 5 minutes or until softened. Add green pepper and hijiki; cook for 5 minutes. Stir in paprika, salt, nutmeg and cayenne. Stir into purée; simmer for 10 minutes. Serve garnished with parsley.

Per serving: 216 calories · 10 g protein · 6 g total fat · 32 g carbohydrate · 6 g fibre (very high)
· 1 g saturated fat · 0 mg cholesterol · 1172 mg sodium
· excellent source iron, folacin · good source vitamin C

Mushroom Veggie Broth

═ ═ ═

You can use any kind of dried mushroom, however I prefer shiitake. The combination of the wine and mushrooms makes for an aromatic broth.

Preparation time: 1½ hours
Makes 2 cups (500 mL)

12	dried mushrooms	12
1 cup	button mushrooms, halved	250 mL
8	dry-packed sun-dried tomatoes	8
1	fennel bulb, chopped	1
2	stalks celery, chopped	2
2	carrots, chopped	2
14	cloves garlic (unpeeled), smashed	14
10	sprigs fresh parsley	10
6	peppercorns	6
1 cup	dry red wine	250 mL

In stockpot, combine 8 cups (2 L) water, dried and button mushrooms, tomatoes, fennel, celery, carrots, garlic, parsley, peppercorns and wine. Bring to boil over medium heat. Reduce heat to low; simmer, uncovered, for 1½ hours. Strain and serve.

Per cup (250 mL): 50 calories · 2 g protein · trace total fat · 11 g carbohydrate
· 2 g fibre (moderate)
· 0 g saturated fat · 0 mg cholesterol · 284 mg sodium

Sea Vegetable Chowder with Pesto

═ ═ ═

*The pesto is made with spinach, basil and parsley instead of the usual basil.
This is a dairy-free recipe but I guarantee it is brimming with flavour.*

Preparation time: 1 hour

Makes 4 servings

3	pieces (6 inch/15 cm each) kombu	3
1 cup	brown rice	250 mL
2 tsp	dried oregano	10 mL
1 tsp	dried marjoram	5 mL
2	medium leeks (white and light green parts), rinsed and cut into ½-inch (1 cm) thick rings	2
1	medium sweet potato, peeled and cut into ½-inch (1 cm) cubes (about 1 cup/250 mL)	1
½ cup	hijiki, soaked in 1 cup (250 mL) water for 5 minutes	125 mL
4	medium carrots, cut into ½-inch (1 cm) thick rounds	4
1 cup	sweet peas	250 mL
1 tsp	sea salt	5 mL
PESTO:		
1 cup	spinach leaves	250 mL
1 cup	mixed basil and parsley leaves	250 mL
1 tbsp	white miso	15 mL
2	cloves garlic, finely chopped	2
½ cup	toasted pine nuts	125 mL
¼ cup	extra virgin olive oil	50 mL

In large pot, bring 12 cups (3 L) cold water, kombu, rice, oregano and marjoram to boil; reduce heat and simmer for 25 minutes. Add leeks, sweet potato, hijiki and carrots; simmer for 20 minutes.

Pesto: Meanwhile, remove stems from spinach, basil and parsley; wash and lightly dry. Place in food processor; add miso, garlic, pine nuts and oil; purée until smooth. (If too thick, add a little water.) Set aside.

Add peas and sea salt to soup; simmer for 5 minutes. Remove kombu. Ladle soup into bowls; spoon 2 tbsp (25 mL) pesto onto each. Serve immediately.

Aunt Jenny's Split Pea and Lentil Soup

An heirloom soup! My grandparents owned a bakery on Phoebe Street in downtown Toronto in the '30s and '40s, and my aunt tells me that there was always a bowl of soup to accompany a piece of bread. The addition of dried shiitake mushrooms and hijiki are my own variation, but I am sure my Zimmerman ancestors would approve of this thick bowlful.

Preparation time: 1¼ hours

Makes 10 servings

1½ cups	dried yellow split peas	375 mL
1 cup	dried green lentils	250 mL
½ cup	dried shiitake mushrooms (about 6)	125 mL
2 tbsp	olive oil	25 mL
2	large onions, chopped	2
3	cloves garlic, minced	3
3	carrots, sliced	3
4	stalks celery, chopped	4
1	sweet potato, peeled and cubed	1
½ cup	hijiki, soaked in 1 cup (250 mL) water for 5 minutes	125 mL
1 tsp	dried thyme	5 mL
1 tsp	salt	5 mL
½ tsp	dried oregano	2 mL
½ tsp	freshly ground black pepper	2 mL
¼ tsp	cayenne pepper	1 mL

Rinse split peas and lentils; place in large pot. Add 10 cups (2.5 L) water; bring to boil. Reduce heat, cover and simmer for 25 minutes.

Meanwhile, place shiitakes in medium bowl; cover with 1½ cups (375 mL) boiling water. Let stand, covered, for 15 minutes or until softened. Drain, reserving water. Squeeze out excess moisture; cut off stems and slice. Set aside.

In large skillet, heat oil over medium-high heat. Cook onions and garlic for 5 minutes or until softened. Stir into split peas along with carrots, celery, potato, hijiki, thyme, salt, oregano, pepper and cayenne. Simmer, stirring often, for 20 minutes or until vegetables are tender. Add reserved shiitake water if desired. Stir in shiitakes.

Split Pea Soup

No ham here! Just a thick pea soup that nourishes the soul. Serve with crusty rye bread.

Preparation time: 1½ hours

Makes 4 to 6 servings

3 tbsp	canola oil	50 mL
1 tsp	dried basil	5 mL
1 tsp	cumin powder	5 mL
½ tsp	freshly ground black pepper	2 mL
½ tsp	ground ginger	2 mL
2 cups	dried split peas	500 mL
½ cup	diced carrots	125 mL
½ cup	diced celery	125 mL
½ cup	diced sweet green pepper	125 mL
1 tbsp	fresh lemon juice	15 mL
1 tbsp	sea salt	15 mL
2 tsp	tamari (approx.)	10 mL
1 tsp	liquid honey	5 mL

In large pot or Dutch oven, heat oil over medium heat. Add basil, cumin, pepper and ginger; stir until fragrant.

Add 10 cups (2.5 L) water; bring to boil. Stir in split peas, carrots, celery, green pepper, lemon juice, salt, tamari and honey; return to boil.

Reduce heat, cover and simmer for 1¼ hours or until peas are softened, stirring often. Season with more tamari if desired.

Per each of 6 servings: 309 calories · 17 g protein · 8 g total fat · 45 g carbohydrate · 6 g fibre (very high) · 1 g saturated fat · 0 mg cholesterol · 901 mg sodium · excellent source folacin · good source iron

Cuban Black Bean Soup

Teresa Rodriguez prepares this hearty soup for the Fred Victor Women's Hostel located in downtown Toronto. Teresa, who came to Canada from Cuba, is very passionate about food. The women at the hostel always appreciate her interesting and delicious meals.

Soaking time: 4 hours

Preparation time: 2 hours

Makes 4 servings

1½ cups	dried black beans	375 mL
5	cloves garlic	5
1	bay leaf	1
2 tbsp	olive oil	25 mL
1	Spanish onion, chopped	1
1	sweet green pepper, chopped	1
1 tsp	each dried oregano and ground cumin	5 mL
1 tsp	freshly ground black pepper	5 mL
2 cups	vegetable stock (page 49) or water	500 mL
2 tbsp	balsamic vinegar	25 mL
½ tsp	salt	2 mL

Rinse beans; soak, covered in cold water, for 4 hours. Drain. In large pot or Dutch oven, cover beans with 8 cups (2 L) water. Cut 2 cloves of the garlic in half; add to beans along with bay leaf. Bring to boil; reduce heat and simmer for 1½ hours or until beans are tender.

Meanwhile, in large skillet, heat oil over medium heat. Mince remaining garlic and add to skillet along with onion, green pepper, oregano, cumin and pepper; cook for 5 minutes or until vegetables are softened.

Stir vegetable mixture into beans along with stock, vinegar and salt; simmer over low heat for 30 minutes. Discard bay leaf.

Per serving: 382 calories · 19 g protein · 9 g total fat · 60 g carbohydrate · 14 g fibre (very high)
· 1 g saturated fat · 0 mg cholesterol · 615 mg sodium
· excellent source iron, folacin · good source vitamin C

Potato and Celery Soup with Celeriac

This smooth, filling soup calls for celeriac, a tough, knobby root. It's often sold caked with dirt so rinse it carefully. Celeriac resembles parsley and celery in flavour and can also be grated raw for salads.

Preparation time: 30 minutes

Makes 8 servings

2 tbsp	extra virgin olive oil	25 mL
2	onions, sliced	2
3	cloves garlic, minced	3
1 tsp	dried thyme	5 mL
1 lb	potatoes (about 3), peeled and cubed	500 g
1	sweet potato, peeled and cubed	1
2 cups	diced celeriac (1 small head)	500 mL
3	stalks celery, sliced	3
6 cups	vegetable stock (page 49) or water	1.5 L
1-½ cups	milk	375 mL
1 tsp	salt	5 mL
¼ tsp	freshly grated or ground nutmeg	1 mL

In large pot or Dutch oven, heat oil over medium heat; cook onions, garlic and thyme for 5 minutes or until softened. Add potatoes, sweet potato, celeriac and celery, stirring to coat.

Add vegetable stock and bring to boil; reduce heat and simmer, covered, for 15 minutes or until vegetables are softened.

Transfer in batches to food processor fitted with metal blade; process until smooth. Return to pot over medium heat. Add milk, salt and nutmeg; cook until heated through.

Per serving: 183 calories · 5 g protein · 5 g total fat · 31 g carbohydrate · 3 g fibre (moderate) · 1 g saturated fat · 3 mg cholesterol · 843 mg sodium

Cabbage Soup

Tart yogurt balances the sweet flavours of cabbage, raisins and apples. A chunky soup, delicately spiced, it always takes me back in time to my childhood.

Preparation time: 50 minutes

Makes 8 servings

1 tbsp	canola oil	15 mL
1	onion, chopped	1
1 tsp	ground cinnamon	5 mL
½ tsp	each ground cloves and allspice	2 mL
¼ tsp	ground nutmeg	1 mL
5 cups	shredded red cabbage (about half a cabbage)	1.25 L
¼ cup	raisins	50 mL
2 tsp	salt	10 mL
2	large tart apples, peeled, cored and sliced	2
1 tsp	freshly ground black pepper	5 mL
1½ cups	plain yogurt	375 mL
2 tbsp	fresh lemon juice	25 mL

In large heavy-bottomed pot or Dutch oven, heat oil over medium-low heat. Cook onion, stirring, for 5 minutes or until softened. Stir in cinnamon, cloves, allspice and nutmeg; cook, stirring, for 2 minutes or until fragrant.

Add cabbage, 6 cups (1.5 L) water, raisins and salt; bring to boil. Reduce heat and simmer, covered, for 30 minutes. Add apples and pepper; simmer for 15 minutes. Remove from heat.

Stir in 1 cup (250 mL) of the yogurt and lemon juice. Dollop 1 tbsp (15 mL) of the remaining yogurt on each serving.

Per serving: 105 calories · 3 g protein · 3 g total fat · 19 g carbohydrate · 3 g fibre (moderate) · 1 g saturated fat · 3 mg cholesterol · 616 mg sodium · good source vitamin C

Chickpea Miso Soup with Chilies and Lemongrass

———

Miso is a paste usually made from fermented soybeans. But it can also be made from chickpeas, which suit the chilies and lemongrass.

Preparation time: 30 minutes

Makes 8 servings

½ cup	chickpea miso (page 7 to 8)	125 mL
1 tbsp	minced fresh gingerroot	15 mL
2 tsp	finely grated lime zest	10 mL
3	stalks lemongrass, halved lengthwise and smashed	3
2	jalapeño peppers, seeded and quartered	2
Pinch	freshly ground black pepper	Pinch
8 oz	firm tofu, rinsed and cut into ½-inch (1 cm) cubes	250 g
2 cups	Swiss chard, stemmed, washed and thickly sliced	500 mL
1 cup	button mushrooms, halved	250 mL
1	sweet red pepper, chopped	1
2	green onions, chopped	2
¼ cup	fresh lime juice	50 mL
¼ cup	chopped fresh coriander	50 mL

In large pot or Dutch oven, stir together 8 cups (2 L) water, miso, ginger, lime zest, lemongrass, jalapeños and pepper; bring to boil. Reduce heat and simmer for 15 minutes. Strain through sieve into another pot.

Add tofu, Swiss chard, mushrooms, red pepper, green onions, lime juice and coriander. Return to heat and simmer for 8 minutes. Serve immediately.

Per serving: 70 calories · 5 g protein · 2 g total fat · 9 g carbohydrate · 2 g fibre (moderate) · trace saturated fat · 0 mg cholesterol · 652 mg sodium · excellent source vitamin C

Tofu Minestrone

My vow to you dear reader: You will never have to throw out a piece of tofu because it's near or past its expiry date. Tofu freezes exceptionally well and suits this one-pot meal superbly.

Preparation time: 25 minutes

Makes 8 servings

8 cups	vegetable stock (page 49) or water	2 L
1	large onion, chopped	1
3	cloves garlic, chopped	3
1	carrot, grated	1
2	stalks celery, sliced	2
1	can (28 oz/796 mL) crushed tomatoes	1
2 tsp	each dried basil and oregano	10 mL
3 cups	penne pasta	750 mL
8 oz	frozen tofu, thawed and crumbled (see page 6)	250 g
1	can (14 oz/398 mL) Romano beans, drained and rinsed	1
¼ cup	chopped fresh parsley	50 mL
¾ tsp	salt	4 mL
¼ tsp	cayenne pepper	1 mL
¼ cup	freshly grated Parmesan cheese	50 mL

In large pot or Dutch oven, heat 1 cup (250 mL) of the stock over medium heat. Add onion and cook for 5 minutes or until softened.

Add garlic, carrot, celery, tomatoes, basil, oregano and remaining stock; bring to boil. Reduce heat and simmer until vegetables are tender, about 10 minutes.

Add pasta; cook until tender, about 10 minutes.

Stir in tofu, beans, parsley, salt and cayenne. Sprinkle each serving with Parmesan.

Per serving: 265 calories · 13 g protein · 4 g total fat · 46 g carbohydrate · 6 g fibre (very high) · 1 g saturated fat · 2 mg cholesterol · 1159 mg sodium · excellent source folacin · good source calcium, iron

Creamy Broccoli Soup

—— —— ——

I love this recipe because there is no waste since both the broccoli stems and florets are used. Use more cayenne for a spicier soup.

Preparation time: 20 minutes

Makes 4 servings

1	bunch broccoli (about 1 lb/500 g)	1
1 tbsp	olive oil	15 mL
1	large onion, chopped	1
1	clove garlic, minced	1
4 cups	plain soy milk	1 L
⅓ cup	chopped fresh coriander or parsley	75 mL
1½ tsp	salt	7 mL
½ tsp	freshly ground black pepper	2 mL
¼ tsp	cayenne pepper	1 mL

Peel broccoli stems and slice. Separate head into small florets.

In large saucepan, heat oil over medium heat. Cook onion and garlic for 5 minutes or until softened.

Reserving ½ cup (125 mL) florets, stir in broccoli and soy milk; bring to boil. Reduce heat and simmer for 10 minutes or until broccoli is tender.

Transfer soup, in batches, to food processor fitted with metal blade and process until smooth. Add coriander, salt, pepper and cayenne; pulse. Return soup to pot, add reserved florets and reheat gently.

Per serving: 157 calories · 11 g protein · 8 g total fat · 14 g carbohydrate · 6 g fibre (very high)
· 1 g saturated fat · 0 mg cholesterol · 920 mg sodium
· excellent source calcium, vitamin C, folacin · good source iron

Miso Soup with Spinach and Sea Vegetables

This tasty soup is made with miso, which resembles a chunky nut butter. The best miso is made from organic beans and grains and is not pasteurized. Never boil the soup because this destroys the miso's enzymes.

Preparation time: 30 minutes

Makes 8 servings

3	pieces (6 inch/15 cm each) kombu	3
1	small onion, chopped	1
1	carrot, thinly sliced	1
Half	sweet red pepper, chopped	Half
8 oz	firm tofu, rinsed and cubed	250 g
1	pkg (10 oz/300 g) fresh spinach, stemmed, washed and chopped	1
½ cup	hijiki, soaked in 1 cup (250mL) water for 5 minutes	125 mL
3 tbsp	mirin	50 mL
1 tsp	minced fresh gingerroot	5 mL
½ cup	barley miso	125 mL
¼ cup	chopped chives	50 mL

In large pot combine 8 cups (2 L) water and kombu; simmer for 20 minutes. Discard kombu and reserve broth.

Meanwhile, in skillet over medium heat, cook onion in ½ cup (125 mL) water for 5 minutes or until softened. Add carrot and red pepper; cook for 5 minutes or until vegetables are softened. Add to broth.

Add tofu, spinach, hijiki, mirin and ginger.

In small bowl, whisk together miso and 1 cup (250 mL) of the soup; stir back into pot. Simmer for 5 minutes or until spinach is just softened. Serve sprinkled with chives.

Per serving: 90 calories · 6 g protein · 3 g total fat · 12 g carbohydrate · 3 g fibre (moderate) · trace saturated fat · 0 mg cholesterol · 756 mg sodium · excellent source folacin · good source iron

---

Potato, Leek and Asparagus Soup

Delicious hot or cold, this hearty soup features kombu (page 12), which flavours the water and turns it into a broth.

Preparation time: 50 minutes

Makes 4 servings

4	pieces (6 inch/15 cm each) kombu	4
3 tbsp	butter	50 mL
3	cloves garlic, minced	3
2	large leeks (white parts only), rinsed and sliced	2
2	stalks celery, chopped	2
2 tsp	chopped fresh dill	10 mL
½ tsp	dried thyme	2 mL
1 lb	small red potatoes, cubed	500 g
8 oz	asparagus, trimmed and cut into 1-inch (2.5 cm) pieces	250 g
1 tsp	salt	5 mL
¼ tsp	freshly ground black pepper	2 mL
1 cup	low-fat yogurt	250 mL

In large pot, combine kombu with 6 cups (1.5 L) water; cook over medium heat for 20 minutes. Discard kombu and reserve broth.

Meanwhile, in large skillet, melt butter over low heat. Add garlic, leeks, celery, dill and thyme; cover and sweat until leeks are softened, about 15 minutes.

Stir leek mixture into broth along with potatoes; bring to boil. Reduce heat and cook, covered, for 8 minutes or until potatoes are tender. Add asparagus, salt and pepper; simmer for 3 minutes or just until asparagus is tender. Remove from heat.

Remove ¼ cup (50 mL) of the broth and let cool slightly. In small bowl, whisk together yogurt and cooled broth; gradually stir into soup.

Per serving: 237 calories · 7 g protein · 10 g total fat · 32 g carbohydrate · 4 g fibre (high) · 6 g saturated fat · 27 mg cholesterol · 749 mg sodium · excellent source folacin · good source calcium, iron, vitamin C

Curried Lentil Soup

Lentils are small, disk-shaped legumes that come in different sizes and colours, such as brown, green and red. Green lentils are the most readily available. This soup can be enjoyed cold or hot.

Preparation time: 40 minutes

Makes 8 servings

2	cans (28 oz/796 mL each) diced tomatoes	2
2 cups	lentils, rinsed	500 mL
1 tbsp	olive oil	15 mL
1 tsp	salt	5 mL
2 cups	coconut milk	500 mL
2 tbsp	butter	25 mL
2	onions, diced	2
4	cloves garlic, minced	4
1 cup	sliced mushrooms	250 mL
1 tsp	minced fresh gingerroot	5 mL
1 tsp	each turmeric, ground coriander and cumin	5 mL
½ tsp	ground cardamom	2 mL
Pinch	cayenne	Pinch

In large pot or Dutch oven, combine 2 cups (500 mL) water, tomatoes, lentils, oil and salt; bring to boil, stirring often. Reduce heat and simmer for 20 minutes, stirring often.

Add coconut milk; cook for 15 minutes.

Meanwhile, in large skillet, melt butter over medium-low heat. Cook onions, garlic, mushrooms, ginger, turmeric, coriander, cumin, cardamom and cayenne for 8 minutes or until onions are golden. Stir into soup.

Cook soup for 5 minutes, stirring often, or until lentils are tender.

Per serving: 371 calories · 16 g protein · 18 g total fat · 42 g carbohydrate · 9 g fibre (very high) · 13 g saturated fat · 8 mg cholesterol · 656 mg sodium · excellent source iron, folacin · good source vitamin C

Leek, Parsnip and Quinoa Soup

═══ ═══ ═══

This dish highlights the sweet taste of parsnips and the creamy texture of quinoa. Members of the onion family, leeks are easy to cook and have a delightful flavour. Be sure to wash them thoroughly to rinse away the sand. Make a slit three-quarters of the way down the centre of the white part (root) and separate the layers (page 69).

Preparation time: 35 minutes
Makes 8 servings

1 tbsp	olive oil	15 mL
1	large leek (white part only), rinsed and thinly sliced	1
1	red onion, halved and thinly sliced	1
3	stalks celery, thinly sliced	3
2	parsnips, peeled and sliced into 1-inch (2.5 cm) rounds	2
6 cups	water	1.5 L
1 cup	well-rinsed quinoa	250 mL
1	can (28 oz/796 mL) tomato purée	1
1 tsp	crushed dried rosemary	5 mL
1 tsp	chopped fresh thyme	5 mL
1 tsp	salt	5 mL

In large pot or Dutch oven, heat oil over medium heat. Cook leek and onion for 5 minutes or until softened. Add celery and parsnips; cook for 5 minutes or until softened.

Add water, quinoa, tomato purée, rosemary and thyme; bring to boil. Reduce heat and simmer for 25 minutes. Stir in salt.

Per serving: 193 calories · 6 g protein · 3 g total fat · 38 g carbohydrate · 6 g fibre (very high)
· trace saturated fat · 0 mg cholesterol · 337 mg sodium
· excellent source iron, vitamin C · good source folacin

Mediterranean Vegetable Chowder

—— —— ——

*A good friend suggested calling this soup a chowder because it was so busy,
so full of ingredients. It's truly a meal in itself.*

Preparation time: 40 minutes

Makes 10 servings

¼ cup	olive oil	50 mL
1	red onion, chopped	1
5	cloves garlic, minced	5
3	Japanese eggplants, cut in ½-inch (1 cm) thick slices	3
3	stalks celery, cut in 1-inch (2.5 cm) thick slices	3
2	yellow or green zucchini, cut in 1-inch (2.5 cm) thick slices	2
1	sweet red pepper, sliced	1
4 cups	vegetable stock (page 49) or water (approx.)	1 L
1	can (28 oz/796 mL) crushed tomatoes	1
¾ cup	chopped pitted black olives	175 mL
2 tbsp	capers	25 mL
1 tbsp	granulated sugar	15 mL
1	can (14 oz/398 mL) artichoke hearts, quartered	1
1 tbsp	red wine vinegar	15 mL
¼ cup	each chopped fresh basil and parsley	50 mL
¼ tsp	each salt and freshly ground black pepper	1 mL

In large pot or Dutch oven, heat oil over medium heat. Cook onion and
garlic for 5 minutes or until softened. Add eggplants, celery, zucchini and
red pepper; cook for 10 minutes or until softened.

Add stock, tomatoes, olives, capers and sugar; bring to boil. Reduce
heat and simmer for 20 minutes. Add more stock if needed.

Add artichokes, vinegar, basil, parsley, salt and pepper; simmer for
5 minutes.

---

*Per serving: 147 calories · 4 g protein · 7 g total fat · 20 g carbohydrate · 6 g fibre (very high)
· 1 g saturated fat · 0 mg cholesterol · 628 mg sodium
· excellent source vitamin C · good source iron, folacin*

Dill and Chickpea Vegetable Broth

After testing this recipe twice, I approached my colleague and maven chef Rhonda Caplan for a taste test to see if it resembled chicken broth. Rhonda, who has been cooking chicken soup since she was five, was open minded and skeptical at the same time (she had never used kombu before). She pronounced this recipe a delicious soup indeed. Instead of discarding the cooked vegetables, purée them and use for soup.

Soaking time: 6 hours

Preparation time: 45 minutes

Makes 11 cups (2.75 L)

1½ cups	chickpeas	375 mL
2	leeks (white parts only), halved, well rinsed and sliced	2
3	pieces (6 inch/15 cm each) kombu	3
4	cloves garlic, halved	4
5	shallots, peeled and quartered	5
1½ cups	button mushrooms, halved	375 mL
2	parsnips, quartered	2
4	carrots, quartered	4
12	peppercorns	12
8	stems fresh parsley	8
½ tsp	each dried marjoram and rosemary	2 mL
½ cup	dry white wine	125 mL
1 tsp	sea salt	5 mL
¼ tsp	freshly ground black pepper	1 mL
½ cup	chopped fresh dill	125 mL

Rinse chickpeas; soak, covered in cold water, for 6 hours. Drain and rinse.

In large stockpot, combine chickpeas, leeks, kombu, garlic, shallots, mushrooms, parsnips, carrots, peppercorns, parsley, marjoram, rosemary, wine and 14 cups (3.5 L) cold water; bring to boil. Reduce heat and simmer, uncovered, for 40 minutes. Add salt and pepper; simmer for 10 minutes.

Strain broth through sieve; discard vegetables. Return broth to pot. Add dill; simmer for 5 minutes. Let cool. (Broth can be refrigerated in airtight containers for up to 1 week or frozen.)

Tip: 1½ cups (375 mL) dried chickpeas = 4 cups (1 L) cooked.

Per cup (250 mL): 11 calories · trace protein · 0 g total fat · 2 g carbohydrate · 0 g fibre · 0 g saturated fat · 0 mg cholesterol · 160 mg sodium

Sweet Potato Coconut Soup

═ ═ ═

Sweet potatoes blend well with coconut milk creating a velvety taste that pleases the palate. They are also a good source of vitamin A. Look for well-shaped potatoes with a smooth, bright skin.

Preparation time: 25 minutes

Makes 6 servings

4	sweet potatoes, cut in 1-inch (2.5 cm) cubes	4
1 tbsp	olive oil	15 mL
2	leeks (white parts only), rinsed and sliced	2
1 tsp	salt	5 mL
½ tsp	freshly ground black pepper	2 mL
1 tbsp	whole wheat flour	15 mL
1-¼ cups	vegetable stock (page 49) or water	300 mL
2 cups	coconut milk	500 mL
½ cup	chopped fresh parsley	125 mL
½ tsp	ground nutmeg	2 mL

Steam potatoes for about 8 minutes or until softened.

Meanwhile, in large pot, heat oil over medium heat. Cook leeks, salt and pepper for 5 minutes or until softened. Stir in flour. Slowly whisk in stock; cook for 5 minutes or until thickened.

Transfer stock mixture to food processor along with potatoes; purée until smooth. Return to pot.

Stir in coconut milk, parsley and nutmeg. Cook for 5 minutes or until heated through.

Per serving: 285 calories · 4 g protein · 19 g total fat · 29 g carbohydrate · 4 g fibre (high) · 15 g saturated fat · 0 mg cholesterol · 540 mg sodium · excellent source iron · good source vitamin C, folacin

New Vegetarian Basics

Pumpkin Soup with Dried Cranberries

═ ═ ═

My husband, Jim, loves pumpkin anything, so I used some leftover pump-kin purée to create this soup. Dried cranberries and green apples give it a tart sweetness.

Preparation time: 30 minutes

Makes 8 servings

1 tbsp	olive oil	15 mL
2	stalks celery, chopped	2
2	tart green apples, peeled and chopped	2
1	onion, chopped	1
1	carrot, chopped	1
½ tsp	minced fresh gingerroot	2 mL
1	can (28 oz/796 mL) pumpkin purée	1
1 cup	dried cranberries	250 mL
1 tsp	sea salt	5 mL
½ tsp	each freshly ground black pepper and cinnamon	2 mL
1 cup	low-fat yogurt	250 mL

In large pot or Dutch oven, heat oil over medium heat. Cook celery, ap-ples, onion, carrot and ginger for 15 minutes, stirring often.

Stir in pumpkin purée, half of the cranberries, salt, pepper, cinna-mon and 6 cups (1.5 L) water; bring to boil. Reduce heat, cover and sim-mer for 10 minutes or until vegetables are tender.

Transfer, in batches, to food processor fitted with metal blade; purée until smooth. Ladle into bowls; garnish each with 2 tbsp (25 mL) yogurt. Sprinkle with remaining cranberries.

Per serving: 140 calories · 3 g protein · 3 g total fat · 29 g carbohydrate · 4 g fibre (high) · 1 g saturated fat · 2 mg cholesterol · 245 mg sodium

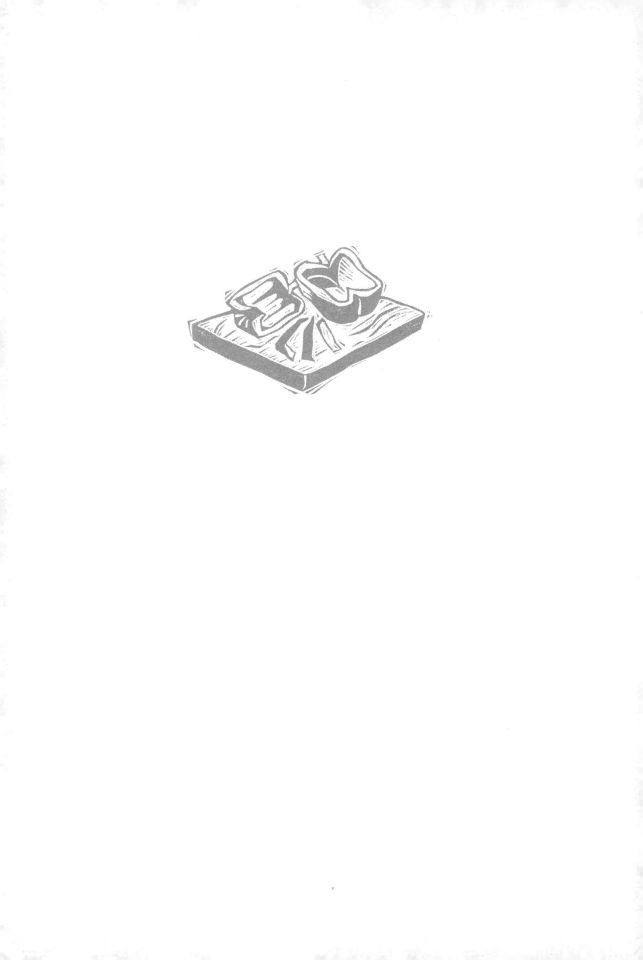

3
Salads and Dressings

Global Salad with Citrus Dressing

Spinach and Lettuce Salad with Goat's Cheese

Spinach, Mustard and Potato Salad

Caesar Salad

Tabbouleh

Waldorf Salad with Tempeh Croutons

Jim's Slaw with Tofu Sour Cream

Beet and Potato Salad

Linguine Salad with Ginger and Garlic

Black Olive Salad with Lentils and Feta

Potato Salad with Salsa Dressing

Beet Salad

Broccoli Black Bean Salad

Calcium Salad

Sea Bean Salad

Mackenzie's Pasta Salad

Marinated Barley Salad

Sweet Potato and Green Bean Salad

Pinto Bean Cashew Rice Salad

Lentil Spinach Salad

Pineapple Beet Salad

continued

Balsamic Vinegar Dressing

Oregano Salad Dressing

Almond Miso Dressing

Tahini Mint Dressing

Tomato Mustard Dressing

Mustard Curry Salad Dressing

Mellow Miso Tofu Dressing

Garlic Dressing

A WORLD OF GREENS

In this chapter and the one following you'll find lots of recipes using leafy greens. There are more green leafy vegetables in our markets than ever before, begging to be tossed in salads, stir-fried, sautéed and stewed. Getting people to eat dark leafy greens has been tough. Many believe the myth that greens lose their nutrients if you cook them for more than a minute or two. The truth is that there are no rules when it comes to cooking greens because they are so varied. Young mustard greens can be eaten raw in a salad while older, tougher greens with stems that are ¼ inch (5 mm) or so thick should be simmered until tender, then drained and sautéed for extra flavour. When you arrive home with your greens, put them in plastic bags and in your refrigerator.

How to Wash Greens

1. Fill a large pot or sink with cold water.
2. Put greens in a strainer or colander.
3. Plunge colander into water and swish greens around. Remove the colander.
4. Look at the water. Does it have grit in it? If so, drain, rinse the pot or sink and repeat the process until the water is free from any residue.

If you are making a salad, you should dry the greens. Water that clings to the leaves will cause any oil-based dressing to slide off and will dilute your tasty salad dressing. Spinners do a great job of drying greens.

How to Cook Greens

There are greens that cook instantly, like spinach, and those that take some time, like kale. If a stem is less than ⅛ inch (3 mm) thick, it can be treated the same as spinach leaves, but cooked a minute longer. When stems are ¼ inch (5 mm) or larger,

I usually strip the leaves, chop the stems and cook them first, adding the leaves only after the stems start to become tender. Thicker stems should be peeled and cooked separately for much longer than the greens.

After years of experimenting, I can honestly say that the best way to cook greens is to parboil them. I bring a large pot of water to a boil, salt it, plunge in my washed spinach, push it under the surface with a big spoon, cook 1 minute, then remove it at once. There are two reasons why I like to cook greens this way. First, you don't need to cover the pot so it's easy to keep an eye on what's cooking. Second, it's easy to stop the cooking at any moment by plunging the greens into a bowl of ice water, which also preserves the colour. Drain and squeeze out the liquid, then chop.

Often I will "finish" the greens by using another cooking method, such as sautéeing or stir-frying. This additional cooking time is very useful if the greens are still not tender, as would be the case with kale, bok choy, collards, rapini and mustard greens.

Greens to Explore

Experiment with this list of greens I use regularly and you're sure to find a new favourite.

arugula	kale
beet top greens	mustard greens
cabbage	radicchio
collard greens	spinach
endive	Swiss chard

Global Salad with Citrus Dressing

━━ ━━ ━━

Around the world with many ingredients! One day I asked my six-year-old daughter Mackenzie to pass me an avocado pear, and when she gave me an avocado and a pear, I was inspired.

Preparation time: 20 minutes
Makes 8 servings

1	avocado, peeled and thinly sliced	1
1	pear, sliced	1
2	oranges, peeled and sectioned	2
4 cups	romaine lettuce, rinsed, torn and dried	1 L
3 cups	spinach, rinsed, stemmed and dried	750 mL
Half	fennel bulb, cored and thinly sliced	Half
Half	red onion, sliced	Half
1	carrot, grated	1
½ cup	roasted pistachio nuts	125 mL
	DRESSING:	
¼ cup	fresh orange juice	50 mL
2 tbsp	olive oil	25 mL
2 tbsp	balsamic vinegar	25 mL
1 tbsp	Dijon mustard	15 mL
½ tsp	mellow miso	2 mL
½ tsp	freshly ground black pepper	2 mL

In large bowl, toss together avocado, pear, oranges, lettuce, spinach, fennel, onion and carrot.

Dressing: In small bowl, whisk together orange juice, oil, vinegar, mustard, miso and pepper until well blended. Pour over salad and gently toss to coat well. Sprinkle with nuts.

Per serving: 182 calories · 4 g protein · 12 g total fat · 19 g carbohydrate · 5 g fibre (high) · 2 g saturated fat · 0 mg cholesterol · 72 mg sodium · excellent source vitamin C, folacin

Spinach and Lettuce Salad with Goat Cheese

━━ ━ ━━

Once, while teaching ten-year-olds in a cooking class, I asked a few to hunt for either spinach or lettuce in the fridge. They brought both. I really liked the combination, so a new recipe was born. This salad has a satisfying crunch and is also excellent stuffed in a pita.

Preparation time: 15 minutes

Makes 4 servings

4 cups	washed torn lettuce	1 L
4 cups	washed torn spinach	1 L
Half	red onion, thinly sliced	Half
1	sweet red pepper, sliced	1
2 oz	mild goat's cheese, crumbled	60 g
	DRESSING:	
¼ cup	olive oil	50 mL
2 tbsp	red wine vinegar	25 mL
2 tbsp	liquid honey	25 mL
1 tbsp	Dijon mustard	15 mL
1	clove garlic, minced	1
Pinch	salt	Pinch

In salad bowl, combine lettuce, spinach, onion and red pepper.

Dressing: In small bowl, whisk together oil, vinegar, honey, mustard, garlic and salt. Pour over salad and toss to coat. Sprinkle with goat's cheese.

Per serving: 240 calories · 5 g protein · 17 g total fat · 19 g carbohydrate · 3 g fibre (moderate) · 3 g saturated fat · 9 mg cholesterol · 164 mg sodium · excellent source vitamin C, folacin · good source iron

Spinach, Mustard and Potato Salad

───── ───── ─────

Capers, little pickled flower buds, add a salty taste to this recipe, much the same way that olives do. If you find the caper flavour too intense, give them a quick rinse. This salad is best dressed minutes before serving.

Preparation time: 30 minutes

Makes 4 servings

4	medium potatoes, peeled and cut into ½-inch (1 cm) cubes (4 cups/1 L)	4
2 tbsp	red wine vinegar	25 mL
2 cups	spinach, washed, torn and dried	500 mL
½ cup	thinly sliced red onion	125 mL
¼ cup	chopped fresh coriander	50 mL
1	sweet green pepper, diced	1
1	small carrot, grated	1
½ cup	toasted pine nuts	125 mL
	DRESSING:	
½ cup	low-fat plain yogurt	125 mL
2 tbsp	Dijon mustard	25 mL
2 tbsp	capers	25 mL
½ tsp	freshly ground black pepper	2 mL

Steam potatoes for 10 minutes or until tender. Transfer to salad bowl. Sprinkle with vinegar; toss to coat. Add spinach, onion, coriander, green pepper, carrot and pine nuts; toss.

Dressing: In small bowl, mix together yogurt, mustard, capers and peppers; add to potatoes and mix gently to coat.

Per serving: 274 calories · 11 g protein · 12 g total fat · 38 g carbohydrate · 7 g fibre (very high) · 2 g saturated fat · 2 mg cholesterol · 229 mg sodium · excellent source iron, vitamin C, folacin

Caesar Salad

Now that anchovy-free Worcestershire-style sauce is available (*The Wiz's or Pick a Pepper*), even a vegetarian can enjoy this delicious dressing. I had this taste-tested by some teenage Caesar salad experts, and no one could tell the difference. You can make it vegan by using soy mayonnaise and soy Parmesan.

Preparation time: 30 minutes

Preheat oven to 400°F (200°C)

Makes 6 servings

1	head romaine lettuce, washed and torn into bite-size pieces	1
½ cup	shaved Parmesan cheese or soy Parmesan (optional)	125 mL
	DRESSING:	
3	dry-packed sun-dried tomatoes, rehydrated (page 42)	3
2	black olives, pitted	2
1	clove garlic, minced	1
2 tbsp	mayonnaise	25 mL
2 tbsp	fresh lemon juice	25 mL
1 tbsp	extra virgin olive oil	15 mL
2 tsp	vegetarian Worcestershire-style sauce	10 mL
1 tsp	Dijon mustard	5 mL
¼ tsp	freshly ground black pepper	1 mL
	CROUTONS:	
2 tbsp	extra virgin olive oil	25 mL
Pinch	salt	Pinch
10	slices French or sourdough baguette	10
1	clove garlic, halved	1

Dressing: In food processor fitted with metal blade, mince together tomatoes, olives and garlic. Add mayonnaise, lemon juice, oil, Worchestershire style sauce, mustard and pepper; process until smooth. (Dressing can be refrigerated in airtight container for up to 3 days.)

Croutons: Mix oil with salt; brush over both sides of bread. Bake on baking sheet in 400°F (200°C) oven, turning once, for 6 minutes or until golden. Immediately rub cut side of garlic over both sides of bread. Cut into 2-inch (5 cm) pieces.

In salad bowl, toss lettuce with dressing to coat. Add croutons, and cheese (if using); toss again.

Per serving: 187 calories · 4 g protein · 12 g total fat · 17 g carbohydrate · 2 g fibre (moderate) · 1 g saturated fat · 3 mg cholesterol · 239 mg sodium · excellent source folacin · good source vitamin C

Tabbouleh

Tabbouleh is made with bulgur, the steamed, dried and crushed berries of wheat which have been a part of our diet from as far back as 1,000 B.C. Nutritionally, 4 oz (125 g) of bulgur has the same nutritional value as a loaf of 100 per cent whole wheat bread.

I have lowered the traditional amounts of parsley and mint in this refreshing salad to allow the cumin and pine nut flavours to surface. Tabbouleh has a wonderful texture and travels extremely well. In a pinch you can use canned chickpeas.

Preparation time: 30 minutes

Chilling time: 1 hour

Makes 6 servings

1½ cups	medium bulgur	375 mL
¼ tsp	salt	1 mL
¼ cup	fresh lemon juice	50 mL
¼ cup	red wine vinegar	50 mL
2	cloves garlic, minced	2
1 tbsp	Dijon mustard	15 mL
½ tsp	ground cumin	2 mL
¼ tsp	each salt and freshly ground black pepper	1 mL
⅓ cup	extra virgin olive oil	75 mL
1 cup	cooked chickpeas (see pages 8 to 9)	250 mL
½ cup	finely chopped red onion	125 mL
¼ cup	each chopped fresh parsley and mint	50 mL
3	tomatoes, diced	3
Half	English cucumber, diced	Half
½ cup	toasted pine nuts	125 mL

In large bowl, stir bulgur with salt; cover with 2¼ cups (550 mL) boiling water. Cover and let stand for 15 minutes or until water is absorbed. Fluff with fork.

Meanwhile, in small bowl, whisk together lemon juice, vinegar, garlic, mustard, cumin, salt and pepper; gradually whisk in oil until combined. Stir into bulgur; cover and refrigerate for at least 1 hour or for up to 12 hours.

Stir in chickpeas, onion, parsley, mint, tomatoes and cucumber. Sprinkle with pine nuts. (Tabbouleh can be covered and refrigerated for up to 2 days.)

Per serving: 368 calories · 11 g protein · 20 g total fat · 43 g carbohydrate · 8 g fibre (very high) · 3 g saturated fat · 0 mg cholesterol · 242 mg sodium · excellent source iron, folacin · good source vitamin C

Waldorf Salad with Tempeh Croutons

Whenever I serve this salad, people always tell me how delicious the croutons are. Tempeh is right at home in this fruit and vegetable salad.

Preparation time: 25 minutes

Makes 6 servings

1 cup	coarsely chopped fennel	250 mL
2	stalks celery, finely chopped	2
1 cup	red seedless grapes, halved	250 mL
1	orange, peeled and sectioned	1
2	tart apples (unpeeled), cut into 1-inch (2.5 cm) chunks	2
½ cup	dried cranberries	125 mL
2 cups	spinach leaves, washed	500 mL
½ cup	tamari-roasted almonds (page 13)	125 mL
CROUTONS:		
2 tbsp	olive oil	25 mL
8 oz	tempeh, cut into ½-inch (1 cm) cubes	250 g
DRESSING:		
½ cup	plain yogurt	125 mL
1	clove garlic, minced	1
½ cup	fresh orange juice (juice of 2 oranges)	125 mL
1 tsp	Dijon mustard	5 mL
½ tsp	grated orange zest	2 mL

Croutons: In large nonstick skillet, heat oil over medium-high heat. Cook tempeh for 8 minutes or until reddish brown on all sides. Drain on paper towel.

In large bowl, combine tempeh croutons, fennel, celery, grapes, orange, apples and cranberries.

Dressing: In separate bowl, whisk together yogurt, garlic, orange juice, mustard and orange zest. Pour over fruit mixture and toss until coated.

Line platter with spinach leaves; top with salad. Sprinkle with almonds.

Citrus Sense

Do you often like to add a wedge of lemon, lime or orange to your sparkling water, fruit juice or iced tea? Or maybe just the peel? Don't use citrus peels unless they are organic! Unless you are using organically grown ingredients, it is very difficult to avoid pesticide residue. The rind retains the many chemicals used in spraying. Many recipes require the zest, or the thin coloured layer of skin, that contains flavourful citrus oils. You can remove it using a zester, or a potato peeler.

Per serving: 305 calories · 12 g protein · 15 g total fat · 37 g carbohydrate · 4 g fibre (high) · 2 g saturated fat · 1 mg cholesterol · 232 mg sodium · excellent source vitamin C, folacin · good source iron

Jim's Slaw with Tofu Sour Cream

━━ ━━ ━━

I developed this tasty dairy-free cole slaw dressing for my husband Jim who is lactose intolerant. The tofu sour cream is just like the real thing!

Preparation time: 15 minutes

Makes 4 servings

⅓ cup	Tofu Sour Cream (see page 87)	75 mL
2 tbsp	balsamic vinegar	25 mL
2 tsp	maple syrup	10 mL
1 tsp	Dijon mustard	5 mL
¼ tsp	each salt and freshly ground black pepper	1 mL
2 cups	thinly shredded red cabbage	500 mL
1	carrot, grated	1
2	green onions, sliced	2
8	asparagus spears, lightly steamed and cut into ½-inch (1 cm) pieces	8

In large bowl, whisk together Tofu Sour Cream, vinegar, maple syrup, mustard, salt and pepper.

Add cabbage, carrot, onions and asparagus; toss until vegetables are coated.

Per serving: 66 calories · 3 g protein · 2 g total fat · 11 g carbohydrate · 2 g fibre (moderate) · trace saturated fat · 0 mg cholesterol · 224 mg sodium · excellent source folacin · good source vitamin C

Tofu Sour Cream

Preparation time: 5 minutes

Makes 1 cup (250 mL)

8 oz	firm tofu, rinsed	250 g
1 tbsp	fresh lemon juice	15 mL
2 tsp	olive oil	10 mL
1 tsp	rice vinegar	5 mL
¼ tsp	salt	1 mL

In food processor, purée tofu until smooth and creamy. Add lemon juice, olive oil, rice vinegar and salt; blend well. Refrigerate for at least 6 hours to thicken before using.

Per tbsp (15 mL): 16 calories · 1 g protein · 1 g total fat · 1 g carbohydrate · 0 g fibre · 0 g saturated fat · 0 mg cholesterol · 37 mg sodium

Beet and Potato Salad

My friend Kathy Barron made this salad for a potluck and then couldn't remember the ingredient amounts she had used because she (an artist) never measures. So, we had to make it together, me with my measuring spoons and cups (the scientist as she calls me). I love how the mint accentuates the feta and beets.

Preparation time: 30 minutes

Makes 4 servings

2	large potatoes	2
2	large beets	2
¼ cup	low-fat plain yogurt	50 mL
2 tbsp	extra virgin olive oil	25 mL
2 tbsp	each red wine vinegar and lemon juice	25 mL
1 tbsp	crushed caraway seeds	15 mL
2	cloves garlic, minced	2
1 tsp	tamari	5 mL
¼ tsp	freshly ground black pepper	1 mL
2 tbsp	chopped fresh mint	25 mL
2	green onions, chopped	2
½ cup	crumbled feta cheese	125 mL

Steam or boil potatoes and beets until tender, about 20 minutes. Peel and slice thinly; place in serving dish.

Meanwhile, in small bowl, mix together yogurt, oil, vinegar, lemon juice, caraway, garlic, tamari and pepper. Pour over beets and potatoes; toss to coat. (Salad can be prepared to this point, covered and refrigerated for up to 2 days.) To serve, sprinkle with mint, onions and feta.

Per serving: 220 calories · 6 g protein · 11 g total fat · 27 g carbohydrate · 3 g fibre (moderate) · 3 g saturated fat · 15 mg cholesterol · 301 mg sodium · good source vitamin C, folacin

Linguine Salad with Ginger and Garlic

Hold the tomatoes! This pasta dish has so much flavour with the garlic, ginger, soy sauce and toasted sesame oil that tomatoes are not necessary.

Preparation time: 25 minutes

Makes 6 servings

1 tsp	dried basil	5 mL
½ tsp	dried rosemary	2 mL
½ tsp	salt	2 mL
8 oz	linguine	250 g
½ cup	hijiki	125 mL
2	cloves garlic, minced	2
1 tsp	minced fresh gingerroot	5 mL
¼ cup	rice vinegar	50 mL
¼ cup	toasted sesame oil	50 mL
3 tbsp	soy sauce	50 mL
1 tsp	hot pepper sauce	5 mL
1	large sweet red pepper, sliced	1
1 cup	chopped green onions	250 mL
1	carrot, grated	1
¼ cup	toasted pine nuts	50 mL

Bring large pot of water to boil; add basil, rosemary and salt. Add linguine; cook until al dente (8 to 10 minutes for dry or 4 to 6 minutes for fresh). Drain.

Meanwhile, soak hijiki in 1 cup (250 mL) cold water for 10 minutes; drain.

In large bowl, whisk together garlic, ginger, vinegar, sesame oil, soy sauce and hot pepper sauce. Add warm pasta and toss to coat. Stir in red pepper, onions, carrot and hijiki. Sprinkle with pine nuts.

Per serving: 295 calories · 8 g protein · 13 g total fat · 38 g carbohydrate · 4 g fibre (high) · 2 g saturated fat · 0 mg cholesterol · 748 mg sodium · excellent source vitamin C · good source iron

Black Olive Salad with Lentils and Feta

———

When my friend Jocie Bussin was visiting us at the cottage, we decided to use up ingredients that were hanging around rather than go shopping. I had more than enough lentils to make soup, so I was ready to try a salad. Jocie is a feta cheese expert and assured me her favourite brand wasn't too salty. The salad was quite the success.

Preparation time: 50 minutes

Makes 6 servings

1½ cups	lentils, rinsed	375 mL
3 cups	romaine lettuce, torn in bite-size pieces, rinsed and dried	750 mL
½ cup	crumbled feta cheese	125 mL
½ cup	thinly sliced red onion	125 mL
Half	English cucumber, halved lengthwise and thinly sliced	Half
½ cup	black olives	125 mL
1	tomato, sliced in wedges	1
	DRESSING:	
½ cup	olive oil	125 mL
¼ cup	balsamic vinegar	50 mL
2 tsp	Dijon mustard	10 mL
2	cloves garlic, minced	2
¼ tsp	salt	1 mL

In medium saucepan, bring 4 cups (1 L) water to boil. Add lentils and return to boil; reduce heat and simmer for 20 minutes. Drain, pressing out extra water. Place in large serving bowl.

Dressing: In small bowl, whisk together oil, vinegar, mustard, garlic and salt. Pour half of the dressing over lentils; let stand for 30 minutes.

Stir in romaine, feta, onion, cucumber, olives and tomato. Pour remaining dressing over top; toss to coat.

Per serving: 392 calories · 15 g protein · 22 g total fat · 36 g carbohydrate · 7 g fibre (very high) · 4 g saturated fat · 9 mg cholesterol · 340 mg sodium · excellent source iron, folacin

Potato Salad with Salsa Dressing

Do you want to cut back on the mayo in your life? Here is a terrific opportunity to take a traditional recipe and use other familiar ingredients. Corn, tomatoes, green onions, salsa (I prefer mild) and carrots makes the dish look especially inviting. You can vary the heat of this salad by using different strength salsas—I prefer mild salsa.

Preparation time: 25 minutes
Makes 8 servings

2½ lb	Yukon Gold potatoes, peeled and cubed (about 10 potatoes)	1.25 kg
Half	red onion, thinly sliced	Half
1 cup	corn kernels	250 mL
2	large tomatoes, chopped	2
2	green onions, sliced	2
1	carrot, grated	1
1 cup	salsa	250 mL
⅓ cup	mayonnaise	75 mL
2 tbsp	fresh lemon juice	25 mL
½ tsp	salt	2 mL
¼ tsp	freshly ground black pepper	1 mL
¼ cup	chopped fresh coriander	50 mL

In large pot, steam potatoes for 10 to 15 minutes or until tender but firm. Place in large bowl along with red onion; let cool.

Stir in corn, tomatoes, green onions and carrot.

In small bowl, stir together salsa, mayonnaise, lemon juice, salt and pepper. Add to potato mixture, toss to coat. Sprinkle with coriander.

Per serving: 207 calories · 4 g protein · 8 g total fat · 33 g carbohydrate · 4 g fibre (high) · 1 g saturated fat · 5 mg cholesterol · 290 mg sodium · good source vitamin C, folacin

Beet Salad

My good friend Tony Flaim is always encouraging me to cook creatively. One day he threw some hard-boiled eggs in with the beets as I was cooking the dressing for this salad. I had to admit the finished dish was delicious and the kids loved eating purple eggs. Serve on a bed of lettuce or spinach.

Preparation time: 25 minutes

Makes 4 servings

2	bunches baby beets	2
6	eggs	6
¼ cup	liquid honey	50 mL
¼ cup	herb vinegar	50 mL
1 tbsp	Dijon mustard	15 mL
1 tsp	salt	5 mL
1	small onion, thinly sliced	1
2 tbsp	chopped fresh thyme, coriander or oregano or a combination	25 mL

Wash, trim and scrape beets; slice thickly. In saucepan, cover beets with 3 cups (750 mL) water; bring to boil. Reduce heat and simmer for 8 minutes or until just tender. Remove beets to bowl to cool; reserve cooking liquid in pan.

Meanwhile, in separate saucepan, cover eggs with water; bring to boil and boil for 9 minutes. Cool in cold water. Peel eggs under cold running water.

Add honey, vinegar, mustard and salt to cooking liquid; bring to boil. Boil for 8 minutes or until reduced to 1 cup (250 mL). Return beets to pot along with eggs, onion and herbs. Chill thoroughly.

Before serving, halve eggs, lengthwise.

Per serving: 221 calories · 11 g protein · 8 g total fat · 28 g carbohydrate · 2 g fibre (moderate)
· 2 g saturated fat · 322 mg cholesterol · 778 mg sodium
· excellent source folacin

Broccoli Black Bean Salad

Every natural foods pantry should have a few cans of black beans ready for use. I serve this fast, easy and delicious salad with many main courses.

Preparation time: 20 minutes
Makes 6 servings

3 cups	blanched broccoli florets	750 mL
1	zucchini, sliced	1
1	sweet red pepper, diced	1
1	small red onion, diced	1
1	can (14 oz/398 mL) black beans, drained and rinsed	1
3 tbsp	olive oil	50 mL
3 tbsp	balsamic vinegar	50 mL
1 tbsp	Dijon mustard	15 mL
1 tbsp	chopped fresh dill	15 mL
½ tsp	salt	2 mL
Pinch	freshly ground black pepper	Pinch

In large bowl, mix together broccoli, zucchini, red pepper, red onion and beans.

In small bowl, whisk together oil, vinegar, mustard, dill, salt and pepper. Pour over salad and toss to combine.

Per serving: 165 calories · 6 g protein · 7 g total fat · 21 g carbohydrate · 5 g fibre (high)
· 1 g saturated fat · 0 mg cholesterol · 342 mg sodium
· excellent source vitamin C, folacin

Calcium Salad

Hijiki, broccoli, apricots and tofu contain significant amounts of calcium, hence the inspiration for the name of this dish. This is also a beautiful salad with contrasting colours and a tangy mustard vinaigrette.

Preparation time: 20 minutes

Makes 4 servings

¼ cup	hijiki	50 mL
2	carrots, sliced	2
2 cups	broccoli florets	500 mL
6 cups	torn mixed salad greens	1.5 L
⅓ cup	quartered dried apricots	75 mL
⅓ cup	toasted pine nuts	75 mL
1 tbsp	olive oil	15 mL
8 oz	firm tofu, rinsed and cut into 1-inch (2.5 cm) cubes	250 g
2	green onions, cut into ½-inch (1 cm) pieces	2
	DRESSING:	
¼ cup	olive oil	50 mL
2 tbsp	Dijon mustard	25 mL
2 tbsp	each red wine vinegar and orange juice	25 mL
1	clove garlic, minced	1
¼ tsp	salt	1 mL
Pinch	freshly ground black pepper	Pinch

Soak hijiki in 1 cup (250 mL) cold water for 10 minutes; drain and transfer to large bowl.

Meanwhile, steam carrots and broccoli together for about 4 minutes or until tender-crisp. Refresh under cold water and drain. Add to hijiki along with salad greens, apricots and pine nuts; toss.

In nonstick skillet, heat oil over medium-high heat. Cook tofu cubes and green onions, turning tofu often, until golden, about 7 minutes. Remove from pan and let cool. Add to salad.

Dressing: In small bowl, whisk together oil, mustard, vinegar, orange juice, garlic, salt and pepper. Pour over salad and gently toss.

Per serving: 351 calories · 12 g protein · 27 g total fat · 22 g carbohydrate · 7 g fibre (very high)
· 4 g saturated fat · 0 mg cholesterol · 400 mg sodium
· excellent source iron, vitamin C, folacin · good source calcium

Sea Bean Salad

━━ ━━ ━━

Arame is the shredded form of a wide-leaf sea grass with a mild aroma and taste. Some say it resembles black angel hair pasta. Arame is precooked before it is dehydrated so it requires very little cooking time. The three types of beans, red onion and celery all contribute to a very attractive salad. And the dressing is so tasty that I often use it for other salads. This recipe can easily be halved.

Preparation time: 20 minutes

Makes 12 to 15 servings

½ cup	arame	125 mL
1	can (14 oz/398 mL) chickpeas	1
1	can (14 oz/398 mL) lentils	1
1	can (14 oz/398 mL) black beans	1
1 cup	corn kernels	250 mL
1 cup	sliced celery	250 mL
1	red onion, halved and thinly sliced	1
1	each sweet yellow and red pepper, finely diced	1
Half	English cucumber, diced	Half
½ cup	chopped fresh coriander	125 mL
	DRESSING:	
½ cup	red wine vinegar	125 mL
¼ cup	fresh lemon juice	50 mL
1	clove garlic, minced	1
2 tsp	Dijon mustard	10 mL
½ tsp	ground cumin	2 mL
½ tsp	salt	2 mL
¼ tsp	freshly ground black pepper	1 mL
½ cup	olive oil	125 mL

Soak arame in 1 cup (250 mL) cold water for 5 minutes; drain. Drain and rinse chickpeas, lentils and black beans. In large bowl, combine beans, arame, corn, celery, onion, yellow and red peppers, cucumber and coriander.

Dressing: In bowl, whisk together vinegar, lemon juice, garlic, mustard, cumin, salt and pepper. Slowly whisk in oil. Pour over bean mixture and toss until thoroughly combined.

Per each of 12 servings: 211 calories · 7 g protein · 10 g total fat · 26 g carbohydrate · 5 g fibre (high) · 1 g saturated fat · 0 mg cholesterol · 319 mg sodium · excellent source vitamin C, folacin · good source iron

---

Mackenzie's Pasta Salad

―――― ―――― ――――

The day my daughter, Mackenzie, discovered black olives was a culinary landmark. My family is always improvising our meals, using whatever ingredients are at hand, and this day there were leftover cherry tomatoes, olives and broccoli. This salad makes a great cold lunch.

Preparation time: 20 minutes

Makes 4 servings

2 cups	penne or rotini pasta	500 mL
2 cups	broccoli florets	500 mL
½ cup	black olives	125 mL
15	cherry tomatoes, halved	15
1	can (19 oz/540 mL) black beans, drained and rinsed	1
½ cup	Garlic Dressing (page 112)	125 mL

In large pot of boiling salted water, cook pasta until just tender, about 10 minutes. Drain and rinse with cold water. Meanwhile, steam broccoli until tender-crisp.

In large bowl, toss together pasta, broccoli, olives, tomatoes, beans and dressing.

Per serving: 428 calories · 16 g protein · 13 g total fat · 63 g carbohydrate · 9 g fibre (very high)
· 2 g saturated fat · 0 mg cholesterol · 490 mg sodium
· excellent source iron, vitamin C, folacin

New Vegetarian Basics

Marinated Barley Salad

———

Barley cooking in a big pot takes me back to my grandmother's kitchen. She lived with my Aunt Jenny and her family and whenever I would visit, I could always count on a cup of strong tea from the samovar and a bowl of deliciously prepared grains. Marinate the grains for at least a half hour. They will absorb the marinade greedily. This salad's flavour improves with time, so let it sit if possible.

Preparation time: 1 hour

Makes 6 servings

1 cup	pearl barley, rinsed	250 mL
2 tbsp	each tamari and toasted sesame oil	25 mL
1 tbsp	mirin	15 mL
2	cloves garlic, minced	2
1 tbsp	olive oil	15 mL
1	red onion, finely chopped	1
2 cups	thinly sliced shiitake mushrooms	500 mL
2	stalks celery, diced	2
¼ cup	chopped fresh coriander	50 mL
Pinch	each salt and freshly ground black pepper	Pinch

In saucepan, bring 3 cups (750 mL) salted water to boil. Add barley and return to boil. Reduce heat and simmer for 50 minutes until barley is tender. Drain and place in large bowl.

In small bowl, whisk together tamari, sesame oil, mirin and garlic; pour half over barley and toss. Set aside.

In large skillet, heat oil over medium-high heat. Cook onion for 5 minutes or until softened. Add mushrooms and celery; cook for 5 minutes, stirring often. Add to barley along with remaining dressing, coriander, salt and pepper; toss well.

Per serving: 218 calories · 4 g protein · 7 g total fat · 35 g carbohydrate · 4 g fibre (high) · 1 g saturated fat · 0 mg cholesterol · 450 mg sodium

Sweet Potato and Green Bean Salad

━━ ━━ ━━

I would like everyone to buy organically grown fruits and veggies that don't need peeling, but this change will take time. So, if you buy commercially-grown produce, peel it. When buying sweet potatoes (high in vitamin A) for this salad, make sure they are firm, well-shaped and have evenly coloured skin that ranges from tan to copper.

Preparation time: 20 minutes

Makes 4 servings

1 lb	sweet potatoes (about 2), peeled and cut into 1-inch (2.5 cm) cubes	500 g
2 cups	green beans, cut into 1½ inch (4 cm) pieces	500 mL
1 cup	corn kernels	250 mL
Pinch	each salt and freshly ground black pepper	Pinch
4	hard-boiled eggs, peeled and quartered	4
2 tbsp	toasted pumpkin or sunflower seeds	25 mL
	BALSAMIC DRESSING:	
⅓ cup	olive oil	75 mL
3 tbsp	balsamic vinegar	50 mL
1	clove garlic, minced	1
½ tsp	granulated sugar	2 mL
¼ tsp	salt	1 mL

Balsamic Dressing: In jar with tight-fitting lid, shake together oil, vinegar, garlic, sugar and salt. (Dressing can be refrigerated for up to 4 days.) Shake again before using.

Steam sweet potatoes for 15 minutes or until tender. Meanwhile, steam green beans for 8 minutes or until tender. Let cool. Place in large bowl. Stir in corn, salt, pepper and ⅓ cup (75 mL) of the dressing, adding more dressing if desired. Arrange eggs on top; sprinkle with seeds.

Per serving: 353 calories · 12 g protein · 21 g total fat · 33 g carbohydrate · 5 g fibre (high)
· 4 g saturated fat · 214 mg cholesterol · 164 mg sodium
· excellent source folacin · good source iron, vitamin C

Pinto Bean Cashew Rice Salad

——— ——— ———

As well as a crunchy salad, this makes a perfect burrito or pita filling. It's a great way to use leftover cooked rice (about 2 cups/500 mL); just reheat it before combining.

Preparation time: 50 minutes

Makes 8 servings

1½ cups	brown rice, rinsed	375 mL
¼ cup	fresh lime juice	50 mL
2 tbsp	Dijon mustard	25 mL
2	cloves garlic, minced	2
½ tsp	each salt and ground cumin	2 mL
¼ tsp	cayenne pepper	1 mL
¼ cup	olive oil	50 mL
2 cups	cooked pinto beans (see pages 8 to 9)	500 mL
1	each sweet red and green pepper, chopped	1
1	large carrot, grated	1
Half	red onion, finely chopped	Half
¼ cup	coarsely chopped fresh coriander	50 mL
½ cup	roasted cashews	125 mL

In medium pot, bring 3½ cups (875 mL) salted water to boil; stir in rice. Cover, reduce heat and simmer for 40 minutes or until tender.

In large bowl, whisk together lime juice, mustard, garlic, salt, cumin and cayenne. Slowly whisk in oil until thoroughly blended. Add pinto beans, red and green pepper, carrot, red onion, coriander and rice; toss until combined. Sprinkle with cashews.

Per serving: 324 calories · 9 g protein · 12 g total fat · 46 g carbohydrate · 7 g fibre (very high)
· 2 g saturated fat · 0 mg cholesterol · 315 mg sodium
· excellent source vitamin C, folacin · good source iron

Lentil Spinach Salad

Lentils are one of the oldest cultivated foods. This combination of spinach, potatoes and lentils in a mild vinaigrette requires only fresh rye bread to complete the meal.

Preparation time: 40 minutes

Chilling time: 30 minutes

Makes 6 servings

1 cup	green lentils, rinsed and picked over	250 mL
5	cloves garlic	5
½ tsp	salt	2 mL
8 oz	mixed sweet and white potatoes, peeled	250 g
⅓ cup	olive oil	75 mL
4 cups	chopped, stemmed, rinsed spinach or Swiss chard	1 L
⅓ cup	red wine vinegar	75 mL
½ cup	thinly sliced red onion	125 mL
1	carrot, grated	1
¼ cup	chopped fresh basil	50 mL
½ tsp	each dried thyme and marjoram	2 mL
¼ tsp	cayenne pepper	1 mL
¼ tsp	each salt and freshly ground black pepper	1 mL

In saucepan pour enough boiling water over lentils to cover by 3 inches (8 cm); soak for 20 minutes. Drain and return to pot.

Cut 2 of the garlic cloves in half; add to pot along with salt. Add enough water to cover and bring to boil; reduce heat and simmer for 12 minutes or until tender. Drain, discarding garlic. Place in large bowl.

Meanwhile, boil or steam potatoes until tender, about 10 minutes. Drain and let cool. Cut into ½-inch (1 cm) cubes. Add to lentils.

Mince remaining garlic. In large skillet, heat 2 tbsp (25 mL) of the oil over high heat; cook garlic until fragrant. Stir in spinach and toss until just wilted. Add 2 tbsp (25 mL) of the vinegar; toss again. Add to lentil mixture along with onion, carrot and basil.

Whisk together remaining oil and vinegar, thyme, marjoram, cayenne, salt and pepper; pour over salad and toss. Refrigerate until chilled.

Per serving: 259 calories · 10 g protein · 13 g total fat · 29 g carbohydrate · 6 g fibre (very high) · 2 g saturated fat · 0 mg cholesterol · 233 mg sodium · excellent source iron, folacin

Pineapple Beet Salad

═ ═ ═

Full of colour and flavour, this light attractive salad just bursts with appeal.

Preparation time: 20 minutes

Chilling time: 15 minutes

Makes 4 servings

2	beets, peeled and grated	2
2	carrots, peeled and grated	2
Half	red onion, grated	Half
1 cup	chopped peeled pineapple	250 mL
1	sweet yellow pepper, diced	1
Half	English cucumber, diced	Half
	DRESSING:	
2 tbsp	fresh lime juice	25 mL
2 tbsp	olive oil	25 mL
2 tbsp	chopped fresh coriander	25 mL
1 tsp	finely grated lime zest	5 mL
1 tsp	chili powder	5 mL

In glass bowl, combine beets, carrots, onion, pineapple, pepper and cucumber.

Dressing: In small bowl, whisk together lime juice, oil, coriander, lime zest and chili powder; pour over salad and toss gently. Refrigerate until chilled.

Per serving: 152 calories · 2 g protein · 7 g total fat · 22 g carbohydrate · 5 g fibre (high) · 1 g saturated fat · 0 mg cholesterol · 54 mg sodium · excellent source vitamin C, folacin

Balsamic Vinegar Dressing

This light dressing goes well with salad greens, but is just as delicious tossed with cooked leafy greens. This recipe can be easily doubled.

Preparation time: 5 minutes
Makes ½ cup (125 mL)

⅓ cup	balsamic vinegar	75 mL
3 tbsp	fresh lime juice	50 mL
1 tbsp	tamari	15 mL
1 tsp	each mirin and rice vinegar	5 mL
¼ tsp	freshly ground black pepper	1 mL

In small bowl, whisk together balsamic vinegar, lime juice, tamari, mirin, rice vinegar and pepper. (Dressing can be refrigerated in airtight container for up to 2 weeks; shake before using.)

Per tbsp (15 mL): 15 calories · 0 g protein · 0 g total fat · 3 g carbohydrate · 0 g fibre · 0 g saturated fat · 0 mg cholesterol · 127 mg sodium

Oregano Salad Dressing

Serve with greens and tomatoes.

Preparation time: 5 minutes
Makes ⅔ cup (155 mL)

¼ cup	red wine vinegar	50 mL
2 tbsp	water	25 mL
2 tbsp	fresh lemon juice	25 mL
2 tbsp	flaxseed oil	25 mL
2 tbsp	chopped fresh dill	25 mL
1 tsp	dried oregano	5 mL
Pinch	freshly ground black pepper	Pinch

In small bowl, whisk together vinegar, water, lemon juice, oil, dill, oregano and pepper. (Dressing can be refrigerated in airtight container for up to 2 days.)

Per tbsp (15 mL): 24 calories · 0 g protein · 3 g total fat · 1 g carbohydrate · 0 g fibre · trace saturated fat · 0 mg cholesterol · 0 mg sodium

Almond Miso Dressing

Serve with fresh vegetables and mini pitas.

Preparation time: 10 minutes
Makes 1 cup (250 mL)

⅓ cup	water	75 mL
¼ cup	chopped green onions	50 mL
3 tbsp	fresh lime juice	50 mL
2 tbsp	flaxseed oil	25 mL
2 tbsp	almond nut butter	25 mL
1 tbsp	white miso	15 mL
1 tbsp	rice vinegar	15 mL
1 tsp	minced fresh gingerroot	5 mL
1 tsp	liquid honey	5 mL
1	clove garlic, minced	1
Pinch	red pepper flakes	Pinch

In food processor or blender, combine water, onions, lime juice, oil, almond butter, miso, rice vinegar, ginger, honey, garlic and red pepper flakes; process until thoroughly blended. (Dressing can be refrigerated in airtight container for up to 2 days.)

Per tbsp (15 mL): 33 calories · trace protein · 3 g total fat · 2 g carbohydrate · 0 g fibre · trace saturated fat · 0 mg cholesterol · 40 mg sodium

Tahini Mint Dressing

As well as a dressing, this also makes a delicious vegetable dip. Serve it with Veggies in a Pita (page 142) or as a dressing for Tofu Neatballs (page 31).

Preparation time: 10 minutes

Makes ¾ cup (175 mL)

½ cup	water	125 mL
3 tbsp	tahini	50 mL
3 tbsp	fresh mint	50 mL
2	cloves garlic, minced	2
2 tbsp	fresh lemon juice	25 mL
1 tbsp	flaxseed oil	15 mL
1 tsp	white miso	5 mL
½ tsp	ground cumin	2 mL
¼ tsp	salt	1 mL

In food processor or blender, combine water, tahini, mint, garlic, lemon juice, oil, miso, cumin and salt; process until thoroughly blended. (Dressing can be refrigerated in airtight container for up to 2 days.)

Per tbsp (15 mL): 34 calories · 1 g protein · 3 g total fat · 1 g carbohydrate · trace fibre · trace saturated fat · 0 mg cholesterol · 66 mg sodium

Tomato Mustard Dressing

—— —— ——

This makes a very good substitute for mayonnaise.

Preparation time: 10 minutes
Makes 2 cups (500 mL)

4 oz	firm tofu, rinsed	125 g
2	cloves garlic, crushed	2
1	small tomato, quartered	1
Quarter	red onion, chopped	Quarter
¼ cup	water	50 mL
2 tbsp	fresh lemon juice	25 mL
2 tbsp	rice vinegar	25 mL
1 tbsp	Dijon mustard	15 mL
1 tbsp	chopped fresh coriander	15 mL
2 tsp	soy sauce	10 mL
¼ tsp	salt	1 mL

In food processor or blender, combine tofu, garlic, tomato, onion, water, lemon juice, rice vinegar, mustard, coriander, soy sauce and salt; process until very smooth. (Dressing can be refrigerated in airtight container for up to 2 days.)

Per tbsp (15 mL): 6 calories · trace protein · 0 g total fat · 1 g carbohydrate · 0 g fibre · 0 g saturated fat · 0 mg cholesterol · 47 mg sodium

Mustard Curry Salad Dressing

━━ ━━ ━━

This dressing adds a lot of power to any salad. For maximum taste, make sure the curry powder is fresh. Try serving with Lentil Pistachio Loaf (page 158) or Curried Parsnip and Bean Burgers (page 152).

Preparation time: 10 minutes

Makes 1 cup (250 mL)

¼ cup	red wine vinegar	50 mL
1 tbsp	fresh lime juice	15 mL
1 tbsp	soy sauce	15 mL
1 tbsp	Dijon mustard	15 mL
1 tsp	granulated sugar	5 mL
1 tsp	curry powder	5 mL
½ tsp	salt	2 mL
¼ tsp	freshly ground black pepper	1 mL
½ cup	extra virgin olive oil	125 mL

In small bowl, whisk together vinegar, lime juice, soy sauce, mustard, sugar, curry powder, salt and pepper. In steady stream, gradually whisk in oil until emulsified. (Dressing can be refrigerated in airtight container for up to 1 week; shake before using.)

Per tbsp (15 mL): 63 calories · 0 g protein · 7 g total fat · 1 g carbohydrate · 0 g fibre · 1 g saturated fat · 0 mg cholesterol · 149 mg sodium

Mellow Miso Tofu Dressing

━━ ━━ ━━

Use this thick dressing for potato or pasta salads because it coats well.

Preparation time: 5 minutes

Makes 2 cups (500 mL)

8 oz	firm tofu, rinsed	250 g
⅓ cup	water	75 mL
¼ cup	mellow miso	50 mL
¼ cup	rice vinegar	50 mL
¼ cup	fresh coriander leaves	50 mL
2 tbsp	toasted sesame oil	25 mL
2 tbsp	tahini	25 mL

In food processor fitted with metal blade, purée together tofu, water, miso, rice vinegar, coriander, oil and tahini until smooth. (Dressing can be refrigerated in airtight container for up to 1 week.)

Per tbsp (15 mL): 23 calories · 1 g protein · 2 g total fat · 1 g carbohydrate · 0 g fibre · trace saturated fat · 0 mg cholesterol · 79 mg sodium

Garlic Dressing

Serve with salad greens, or as a topping for baked potatoes, French bread or sliced vegetables.

Preparation time: 70 minutes

Preheat oven to 325°F (160°C)

Makes 1 cup (250 mL)

2	whole garlic bulbs	2
2 tbsp	olive oil	25 mL
¼ cup	water	50 mL
¼ cup	extra virgin olive oil	50 mL
1 tbsp	balsamic vinegar	15 mL
1 tbsp	red wine vinegar	15 mL
½ tsp	liquid honey	2 mL
Pinch	each salt and freshly ground black pepper	Pinch

Place each garlic bulb on square of foil; drizzle each with 1 tbsp (15 mL) oil. Seal to form 2 packets. Roast in 325°F (160°C) oven for 1 hour or until bulb is easily pierced by fork. Let cool enough to handle; squeeze out pulp into food processor. Add water; process to blend.

Add oil, balsamic and wine vinegars, honey, salt and pepper; purée until creamy.

Per tbsp (15 mL): 57 calories · trace protein · 5 g total fat · 3 g carbohydrate · 0 g fibre · 1 g saturated fat · 0 mg cholesterol · 1 mg sodium

4
Side Dishes

▬ ▬ ▬

Roasted Vegetables

Pumpkin Sesame Green Beans

Acorn Squash with Cherries and Mint

Baked Squash and Fruit

Greens and Black Beans

Greens with Chilies, Cranberries and Almonds

Beet Greens with Celeriac and Sweet Potatoes

Hijiki with Carrots and Sesame Seeds

Creamy Herbed Polenta

Kombu Orange Rice

Boiled Black Beans

Refried Black Beans

Barley with Cranberries

Rosemary Dill Potatoes

Portobello Baked Potato

Grilled Tofu

Fruit and Tomato Chutney

Roasted Vegetables

━━ ━━ ━━

Roasted vegetables go well with everything! Serve this with rice or noodles, or use it as an amazing sandwich filler.

Preparation time: 15 minutes
Preheat oven to 350°F (180°C)
Cooking time: 45 minutes
Makes 4 servings

1	each sweet red and green pepper, cut into 1-inch (2.5 cm) pieces	1
2	onions, peeled and cut into eighths with root intact	2
3	zucchini, cut into ½-inch (1 cm) thick slices	3
1	large potato, peeled and cut into ½-inch (1 cm) cubes	1
2 cups	cubed (½ inch/1 cm) acorn squash	500 mL
6	cloves garlic	6
½ tsp	dried rosemary	2 mL
2 tbsp	olive oil	25 mL
1 tbsp	rice vinegar	15 mL
1 tsp	tamari	5 mL
½ tsp	each salt and freshly ground black pepper	2 mL

In large bowl, combine red and green peppers, onions, zucchini, potato, squash, garlic and rosemary. In small bowl, whisk together oil, rice vinegar, tamari, salt and pepper; pour over vegetables and toss to coat.

Spread vegetables in single layer on large baking sheet. Roast in 350°F (180°C) oven, stirring once, for about 45 minutes or until tender and browned.

Per serving: 189 calories · 4 g protein · 7 g total fat · 31 g carbohydrate · 6 g fibre (very high) · 1 g saturated fat · 0 mg cholesterol · 381 mg sodium · excellent source vitamin C · good source folacin

Pumpkin Sesame Green Beans

Along with the garlic and pumpkin seeds, rosemary transforms ordinary green beans into an exceptional dish.

Preparation time: 15 minutes

Makes 4 servings

4 cups	green beans, trimmed	1 L
2 tbsp	olive oil	25 mL
¼ cup	pumpkin seeds	50 mL
2 tbsp	sesame seeds	25 mL
2	cloves garlic, minced	2
½ tsp	crushed dried rosemary	2 mL
Pinch	each salt and freshly ground black pepper	Pinch

In large pot of boiling salted water, cook beans for 5 minutes or until just tender. Drain.

In large skilllet, heat oil over medium heat. Add pumpkin seeds; cook until brown, about 5 minutes. Add sesame seeds, garlic and rosemary; cook for 2 minutes. Add green beans; cook until heated through, about 3 minutes. Season with salt and pepper.

Per serving: 202 calories · 8 g protein · 16 g total fat · 11 g carbohydrate · 5 g fibre (high) · 2 g saturated fat · 0 mg cholesterol · 109 mg sodium · excellent source iron · good source folacin

Acorn Squash with Cherries and Mint

The sweetness of cherries and raisins is tempered by the orange juice and rind to bake into melt-in-your-mouth squash.

Preparation time: 10 minutes

Preheat oven to 400°F (200°C)

Cooking time: 45 minutes

Makes 4 servings

1	acorn squash, halved, seeded and fibres removed	1
¼ cup	fresh orange juice	50 mL
¼ cup	dried cherries, halved	50 mL
2 tbsp	raisins	25 mL
2 tsp	finely grated orange zest	10 mL
1 tbsp	chopped fresh mint	15 mL

Place squash, cut side up, in 13- x 9-inch (3 L) baking dish.

In measuring cup, stir together orange juice, cherries, raisins and orange zest; divide between squash halves.

Cover with foil and bake in 400°F (200°C) oven for about 45 minutes or until fork-tender. Sprinkle with mint.

Per serving: 89 calories · 1 g protein · 0 g total fat · 23 g carbohydrate · 4 g fibre (high)
· 0 g saturated fat · 0 mg cholesterol · 4 mg sodium
· good source vitamin C

Baked Squash and Fruit

—— —— ——

Apples and pears mesh well with the texture and taste of baked squash in this appealing dish. Butternut squash is tan-coloured and somewhat elongated with a thick neck and bell-shaped bottom. Those with some stem still attached will keep longer. It is available year round and weighs between 1 to 3 lb (500 g to 1.5 kg).

Preparation time: 15 minutes

Preheat oven to 400°F (200°C)

Cooking time: 40 minutes

Makes 6 servings.

1	butternut squash	1
½ cup	pine nuts	125 mL
2 tbsp	olive oil	25 mL
½ tsp	each salt and freshly ground black pepper	2 mL
2	apples, quartered and cored	2
2	pears, quartered and cored	2
1 tbsp	fresh lemon juice	15 mL

Peel and halve squash; scoop out seeds and fibres. Cut into large chunks. Place on baking sheet; toss with pine nuts, oil, salt and pepper. Bake in 400°F (200°C) oven for 15 minutes.

In large bowl, toss apples and pears with lemon juice; add to squash. Bake for 25 minutes, stirring once, or until everything is fork-tender.

Per serving: 214 calories · 5 g protein · 12 g total fat · 29 g carbohydrate · 6 g fibre (very high) · 2 g saturated fat · 0 mg cholesterol · 196 mg sodium · good source iron, vitamin C

Greens and Black Beans

━━ ━━ ━━

I love the satisfying taste of molasses mixed with mustard. It's well suited to black beans, which when mixed with leafy greens makes a delicious combo—either hot or cold. Serve on rice.

Preparation time: 15 minutes
Makes 2 servings

3 cups	chopped stemmed washed Swiss chard (about half a bunch)	750 mL
2 cups	cooked black beans	500 mL
½ tsp	minced fresh gingerroot	2 mL
3 tbsp	Barbados molasses	50 mL
1 tbsp	each Dijon mustard and tamari	15 mL
1 tsp	rice vinegar	5 mL

In large saucepan, bring 2 cups (500 mL) water to boil; stir in Swiss chard and cook for 5 minutes or until tender. Drain, reserving ¼ cup (50 mL) water.

Return Swiss chard to pan. Add black beans and ginger; simmer for 2 minutes.

Stir in molasses, mustard, tamari, rice vinegar and reserved water; cook until heated through.

Per serving: 333 calories · 18 g protein · 1 g total fat · 65 g carbohydrate · 11 g fibre (very high)
· trace saturated fat · 0 mg cholesterol · 702 mg sodium
· excellent source iron, folacin · good source calcium

Greens with Chilies, Cranberries and Almonds

━━ ━━ ━━

We all know we should be eating more leafy greens, and this dish makes it deliciously easy. Swiss chard, collard greens and spinach are coated in a fragrant sauce that's accented by garlic, leeks and chilies.

Preparation time: 35 minutes

Makes 4 servings

¼ cup	dried cranberries	50 mL
1	bunch each (1 lb/500 g each) Swiss chard, collard greens and spinach, stemmed, washed and shredded (about 5 cups/1.25 L each)	1
2 tbsp	olive oil	25 mL
3	cloves garlic, minced	3
1	large leek (light part only), washed and sliced	1
2	serrano chilies, seeded and finely chopped	2
1 cup	cooked chickpeas	250 mL
1	carrot, grated	1
1 cup	vegetable broth or water	250 mL
¼ cup	chopped fresh coriander	50 mL
1 tsp	finely chopped fresh gingerroot	5 mL
½ tsp	each ground cumin and salt	2 mL
½ cup	tamari-roasted almonds (page 13)	125 mL

In small bowl, cover cranberries with ½ cup (125 mL) boiling water; soak for 5 minutes. Drain, reserving water; set aside.

Meanwhile, steam Swiss chard until just wilted, about 5 minutes; squeeze out excess water and chop coarsely. Repeat with collard greens, cooking for 8 minutes. Repeat with spinach, cooking for 3 minutes.

In large skillet, heat oil over medium heat; cook garlic, leek and chilies until softened, about 5 minutes.

Reduce heat to low. Add chickpeas, carrot, broth, coriander, ginger, cumin, salt and reserved cranberry water; stir well to combine and cook for 2 minutes.

Add Swiss chard, collard greens and spinach; cook until moisture is evaporated, about 7 minutes. Stir in cranberries and almonds.

Per serving: 342 calories · 14 g protein · 18 g total fat · 38 g carbohydrate · 10 g fibre (very high) · 2 g saturated fat · 0 mg cholesterol · 928 mg sodium · excellent source calcium, iron, vitamin C, folacin

Beet Greens with Celeriac and Sweet Potatoes

━━ ━━ ━━

Nothing pleases me more than buying fresh organic beets complete with their leaves. When buying celeriac buy small ones because larger ones have a tendency to taste woody.

Preparation time: 30 minutes

Makes 4 servings

1 tbsp	olive oil	15 mL
1	red onion, diced	1
1 tsp	chopped fresh thyme	5 mL
3 cups	beet greens, washed, stemmed and chopped (1 bunch)	750 mL
2 cups	chopped (1 inch/2.5 cm cubes) celeriac (about 1 lb/500 g)	500 mL
1	large sweet potato, peeled and chopped into 1-inch (2.5 cm) cubes	1
½ cup	vegetable stock or soy milk	125 mL
½ tsp	each sea salt and freshly ground black pepper	2 mL
½ cup	toasted pumpkin seeds	125 mL

In large skillet, heat oil over medium heat; cook onion and thyme for 5 minutes or until softened. Add beet greens; sauté until bright green, about 3 minutes. Set aside.

Steam celeriac for 5 minutes or until tender; add to greens. Using same pot, steam sweet potato for 5 minutes or until tender; add to beet green mixture.

Stir in stock, salt and pepper; simmer for 10 minutes or until heated through. Sprinkle with pumpkin seeds.

Per serving: 312 calories · 14 g protein · 16 g total fat · 34 g carbohydrate · 9 g fibre (very high) · 3 g saturated fat · 0 mg cholesterol · 487 mg sodium · excellent source iron, folacin · good source vitamin C

Hijiki with Carrots and Sesame Seeds

This salad is part of my comfort foods collection. It is easy to prepare, very satisfying and goes well with grain dishes. Hijiki, my favourite sea vegetable, is a good source of calcium.

Preparation time: 25 minutes
Makes 4 servings

1 cup	hijiki	250 mL
¼ cup	sesame seeds	50 mL
1 tbsp	toasted sesame oil	15 mL
2	onions, chopped	2
1	carrot, grated	1
¼ cup	mirin	50 mL
2 tbsp	tamari	25 mL
1 tbsp	brown rice syrup	15 mL

Cover hijiki with cold water; let soak for 5 minutes. Drain.

Meanwhile, in dry skillet, roast sesame seeds over medium heat for 5 minutes, stirring often. Set aside.

In skillet, heat oil over medium heat; cook onions for 5 minutes or until softened. Add carrot, hijiki, mirin, tamari and rice syrup; simmer for 10 minutes. Top with sesame seeds. Serve hot or cold.

Per serving: 187 calories · 6 g protein · 9 g total fat · 22 g carbohydrate · 3 g fibre (moderate) · 1 g saturated fat · 0 mg cholesterol · 894 mg sodium · excellent source iron · good source calcium

Creamy Herbed Polenta

━━ ━━ ━━

Cornmeal is the basis for comforting polenta, a versatile dish that suits any main course. This version studded with onion and mushrooms is my friend Kate Gammal's contribution.

Preparation time: 25 minutes

Makes 4 servings

2 tbsp	olive oil	25 mL
Half	red onion, chopped	Half
3	cloves garlic, minced	3
3 cups	sliced mushrooms	750 mL
6 cups	vegetable stock (page 49)	1.5 L
1½ cups	cornmeal	375 mL
½ cup	chopped fresh coriander	125 mL
¼ cup	chopped fresh basil	50 mL
¼ cup	freshly grated Parmesan cheese	50 mL
¼ tsp	freshly ground black pepper	1 mL

In large pot, heat oil over medium heat; cook onion and garlic for 5 minutes or until softened. Add mushrooms; cook for 5 minutes.

Stir in stock and bring to boil. Gradually whisk in cornmeal; cook, stirring constantly, for about 15 minutes or until smooth and thick enough to mound stiffly on spoon. Mix in coriander, basil, Parmesan and pepper. Serve immediately.

Tip: For a creamier polenta, substitute 2 cups (500 mL) milk or cream for the same amount of stock.

Per serving: 336 calories · 9 g protein · 11 g total fat · 51 g carbohydrate · 4 g fibre (high)
· 2 g saturated fat · 5 mg cholesterol · 1070 mg sodium
· good source folacin

Kombu Orange Rice

Kombu is the principal sea vegetable used in dashi, the traditional Japanese soup stock. It contributes a deep, robust flavour to any cooking water and infuses this rice dish with a delicate flavour.

Preparation time: 20 minutes

Makes 4 servings

½ cup	fresh orange juice	125 mL
2 tsp	grated orange zest	10 mL
½ tsp	salt	2 mL
2	pieces (6 inch/15 cm each) kombu	2
1 cup	rinsed basmati rice	250 mL
¼ cup	coarsely chopped tamari-roasted almonds (page 13)	50 mL

In small saucepan, combine 1½ cups (375 mL) water, orange juice and zest, salt and kombu; bring to boil. Stir in rice; return to boil. Reduce heat and cook, covered, for 15 minutes or until liquid is absorbed. Discard kombu. Serve sprinkled with almonds.

Per serving: 236 calories · 6 g protein · 5 g total fat · 42 g carbohydrate · 1 g fibre · 1 g saturated fat · 0 mg cholesterol · 417 mg sodium

Boiled Black Beans

━━ ━━ ━━

Enjoy these beans and vegetables in broth, or drain and use in *Refried Black Beans (page 127)*. The kombu will not need to be discarded because it dissolves if cooked for an hour and a half as it is in this recipe. Cooking time will vary with the age of the bean. The older the bean, the longer it will take to cook.

Preparation time: 1½ hours

Makes 5 cups (1.25 L)

2 cups	black beans, rinsed	500 mL
4	pieces (6 inch/15 cm each) kombu	4
2	carrots, thickly sliced	2
1	red onion, quartered	1
4	cloves garlic, halved	4
1 tbsp	ground cumin	15 mL
1 tsp	salt	5 mL

In large pot, cover beans with 6 cups (1.5 L) water; soak for 5 hours. Drain and return to pot. Add 10 cups (2.5 L) water and kombu; bring to boil. Skim off foam.

Add carrots, onion and garlic; reduce heat and simmer for 1 hour. Stir in cumin and salt; cook for 30 minutes or until beans are very soft. Add more water if necessary to keep beans covered.

Per cup (250 mL): 318 calories · 20 g protein · 2 g total fat · 59 g carbohydrate · 14 g fibre (very high) · trace saturated fat · 0 mg cholesterol · 485 mg sodium · excellent source iron, folacin

Refried Black Beans

―― ― ――

A good friend who had just returned from Central America insisted that boiled beans must be fried to be called "refried." I bow to the culinary pressure. Serve these in burritos, salads, omelettes and tacos.

Preparation time: 15 minutes

Makes 6 servings

2 tbsp	olive oil	25 mL
1	onion, finely chopped	1
5 cups	cooked black beans	1.25 L
2 cups	bean cooking liquid	500 mL
¼ cup	chopped fresh coriander	50 mL
1 tsp	chopped fresh dill	5 mL
1	jalapeño pepper, seeded and minced	1
1 tsp	salt	5 mL
½ tsp	freshly ground black pepper	2 mL

In large skillet, heat oil over medium heat; cook onion for 5 minutes or until softened.

Add beans and their cooking liquid, coriander, dill, jalapeño, salt and pepper; simmer for 7 minutes or until liquid has been reduced to desired consistency. Remove 1½ cups (375 mL) and mash; stir back into pan.

Tip: If you prefer a less chunky texture, mash more than the 1½ cups (375 mL) suggested.

Per serving: 237 calories · 13 g protein · 5 g total fat · 36 g carbohydrate · 9 g fibre (very high) · 1 g saturated fat · 0 mg cholesterol · 386 mg sodium · excellent source folacin · good source iron

Barley with Cranberries

━━ ━━ ━━

Barley has a pleasant, chewy texture and a satisfying taste. I like combining it with cranberries because their bright colour and tangy bite complement barley perfectly.

Preparation time: 40 minutes

Makes 4 servings

2 tsp	canola oil	10 mL
1 cup	pearl barley	250 mL
4 cups	apple juice	1 L
1	cinnamon stick	1
½ cup	dried cranberries, halved	125 mL

In medium saucepan, heat oil. Add barley and toast, stirring, for 5 minutes or until fragrant.

Add apple juice and cinnamon stick; bring to boil. Reduce heat, cover and cook until barley is tender and liquid has almost been absorbed, about 40 minutes.

Add cranberries; simmer, uncovered and stirring, for 8 minutes. Discard cinnamon stick.

Per serving: 355 calories · 3 g protein · 3 g total fat · 80 g carbohydrate · 5 g fibre (high) · trace saturated fat · 0 mg cholesterol · 12 mg sodium · excellent source vitamin C · good source iron

Rosemary Dill Potatoes

Rosemary is a herb with pine-shaped, pointed leaves that impart the most fragrant of aromas when crushed. Feathery dill has plenty of soft, green spikes. Together they add a lot of flavour without a lot of fat.

Preparation time: 10 minutes

Preheat oven to 400°F (200°C)

Cooking time: 40 minutes

Makes 6 servings

2	large sweet potatoes (unpeeled), cut into ½-inch (1 cm) thick slices	2
6	small red potatoes (unpeeled), halved	6
2 tbsp	olive oil	25 mL
½ tsp	crushed dried rosemary	2 mL
¼ tsp	dried dillweed	1 mL
¼ tsp	each salt and freshly ground black pepper	1 mL

Place potatoes in single layer on ungreased baking sheet.

In small bowl, mix together oil, rosemary, dill, salt and pepper; brush over potatoes.

Bake in 400°F (200°C) oven, turning once, for 40 minutes or until fork-tender.

Per serving: 224 calories · 4 g protein · 5 g total fat · 43 g carbohydrate · 4 g fibre (high) · 1 g saturated fat · 0 mg cholesterol · 112 mg sodium · good source iron, vitamin C

Portobello Baked Potato

=== === ===

When I worked at a health spa in Ontario, we were always baking potatoes, scooping out the centres and adding tasty ingredients such as dill, mushrooms and onions. Tofu and tamari were my contributions.

Preparation time: 15 minutes

Preheat oven to 300°F (150°C)

Cooking time: 15 minutes

Makes 2 servings

1 tbsp	olive oil	15 mL
1	onion, chopped	1
1	clove garlic, minced	1
1½ cups	chopped portobello mushrooms (about 2)	375 mL
1	sweet red pepper, chopped	1
1 tbsp	tamari	15 mL
1 tsp	mirin	5 mL
½ tsp	dried basil	2 mL
8 oz	firm tofu, rinsed	250 g
1 tbsp	chopped fresh dill	15 mL
¼ tsp	each salt and freshly ground black pepper	1 mL
2	large baked potatoes	2

In large skillet, heat oil over medium heat; cook onion and garlic for 5 minutes or until softened. Add mushrooms, red pepper, tamari, mirin and basil; cook for 5 minutes or until vegetables are softened. Set aside.

In food processor, purée together tofu, dill, salt and pepper until smooth.

Cut baked potatoes in half lengthwise and scoop out insides, leaving ¼-inch (5 mm) thick shell. Add potato to tofu mixture; pulse until combined. Stir in all but ½ cup (125 mL) of vegetable mixture. Stuff back into potato shells; top each with ¼ cup (50 mL) vegetable mixture. Bake in 300°F (150°C) oven for 15 minutes or until heated through.

Tip: Bake potatoes in a 425°F (220°C) oven for 45 to 60 minutes or until tender.

Per serving: 373 calories · 16 g protein · 12 g total fat · 54 g carbohydrate · 7 g fibre (very high)
· 2 g saturated fat · 0 mg cholesterol · 819 mg sodium
· excellent source iron, vitamin C, folacin · good source calcium

Grilled Tofu

This recipe includes a delicious marinade that permeates every pore of the tofu. Serve the tofu on kaiser or onion buns, add it to salads or toss it with noodles.

Preparation time: 35 minutes
Preheat grill to medium-high
Cooking time: 4 minutes
Makes 4 servings

¼ cup	each soy sauce and mirin	50 mL
2 tbsp	toasted sesame oil	25 mL
1 tbsp	rice vinegar	15 mL
3	cloves garlic, minced	3
1 tsp	minced fresh gingerroot	5 mL
1 lb	firm tofu, rinsed	500 g

In 13- x 9-inch (3 L) glass baking dish, mix together soy sauce, mirin, sesame oil, rice vinegar, garlic and ginger. Slice tofu into ¼-inch (5 mm) thick slices; add to dish and marinate for 30 minutes at room temperature or for up to 2 hours in refrigerator.

Cook tofu on greased grill, turning once, for 4 minutes, brushing with remaining marinade.

Per serving: 154 calories · 10 g protein · 10 g total fat · 6 g carbohydrate · 1 g fibre · 1 g saturated fat · 0 mg cholesterol · 783 mg sodium · good source calcium, folacin

Fruit and Tomato Chutney

━━ ━━ ━━

I love chutney and use it more like a side dish than a condiment. This all-purpose chutney is exceptional. Try it with Orange Garlic Miso Tempeh (page 173) or Cheesy Vegetable Bean Burritos (page 154) for a real kick.

Preparation time: 30 minutes

Cooking time: 1 to 1½ hours

Makes 6 cups (1.5 L)

2 cups	apple cider vinegar	500 mL
1½ cups	liquid honey	375 mL
½ cup	molasses	125 mL
2	cloves garlic, minced	2
1 tbsp	sea salt	15 mL
1 tbsp	grated fresh gingerroot	15 mL
1 tsp	ground cinnamon	5 mL
2 tbsp	mustard seeds	25 mL
1 tsp	ground cloves	5 mL
1 tsp	ground coriander	5 mL
½ tsp	freshly ground black pepper	2 mL
1 cup	raisins	250 mL
1 cup	chopped dried figs	250 mL
4	medium tomatoes, coarsely chopped	4
4	medium apples, chopped	4
3	medium pears, chopped	3

In large heavy saucepan, combine vinegar, honey, molasses, garlic, salt, ginger, cinnamon, mustard seeds, cloves, coriander and pepper; cook over medium heat, stirring constantly, for 10 minutes.

Add raisins, figs, tomatoes, apples and pears; bring to boil. Cover, reduce heat and simmer for 1 to 1½ hours or until thickened. Transfer to airtight jars. Refrigerate for up to 1 month.

Per tbsp (15 mL): 40 calories · 0 g protein · 0 g total fat · 10 g carbohydrate · 1 g fibre · 0 g saturated fat · 0 mg cholesterol · 74 mg sodium

---

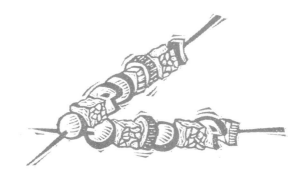

5
Main Courses

Root Vegetable Casserole

Sweet Potato Celeriac Pie

Soba Noodles with Red Onions, Black Beans and Kale

Veggies in a Pita

Sun-Dried Tomato Risotto with Garlic and Greens

Japanese Eggplant with Miso and Curry Paste

Marinated Gourmet Rice with Veggies

Tri-Colour Peppers Stuffed with Chickpeas, Mint and Pine Nuts

Basmati Burger Pockets with Coriander Yogurt Sauce

Curried Parsnip and Bean Burgers

Cheesy Vegetable Bean Burritos

Great Northern Bean Cakes

Black Bean Quinoa Burgers

Lentil Pistachio Loaf

Bean and Pepper Pie

Quinoa Chili

Stir-Fried Tofu with Vegetables in Curried Almond Butter Sauce

Tofu Nuggets with Swiss Chard

Tofu with Leeks and Peanut Butter

Tofu Lasagna

Tofu Turkey with Stuffing, Mushroom Gravy and Cranberry Sauce

Orange Garlic Miso Tempeh

continued

Tempeh Cabbage Rolls
Swiss Chard Rolls with Tempeh Filling
Tempeh Kebabs
Tamarind Tempeh Buckwheat Loaf
Baked Tempeh and Rice Noodle Salad with Hot Sauce
Tempeh Burgers

Versatile Sauces:
All-Purpose Sauce
Sesame Seed Sauce
Barbecue Sauce
100,000 Island Sauce

Root Vegetable Casserole

This hearty casserole fills you up with flavour. When buying parsnips, look for small or medium-size ones that are smooth, firm and free of blemishes. They have a sweet, nutty flavour that blends well with leeks, carrots and celeriac.

Preparation time: 40 minutes

Preheat oven to 400°F (200°C)

Cooking time: 45 minutes

Makes 4 servings

3 tbsp	olive oil	50 mL
3	leeks (white and light green parts only) rinsed and sliced ½-inch (1 cm) thick	3
4	large carrots, thinly sliced	4
4	large parsnips, peeled (optional) and thinly sliced	4
1	small celeriac, washed, peeled and chopped into 1-inch (2.5 cm) cubes	1
1 tbsp	chopped fresh dill or parsley	15 mL
½ tsp	sea salt	2 mL
½ tsp	freshly ground black pepper	2 mL
1½ cups	plain soy milk	375 mL
½ cup	grated Cheddar cheese	125 mL
½ cup	dry bread crumbs	125 mL

In large skillet, heat oil over medium-high heat; cook leeks for 10 minutes. Add carrots, parsnips, celeriac and dill; sauté for 5 minutes. Add salt and pepper. Transfer to 8-cup (2 L) casserole dish.

Pour soy milk over vegetables. Combine cheese with bread crumbs; sprinkle over top. Cover and bake in 400°F (200°C) oven for 15 minutes. Uncover and bake for 30 minutes longer or until topping is golden brown.

Per serving: 472 calories · 13 g protein · 18 g total fat · 70 g carbohydrate · 13 g fibre (very high) · 5 g saturated fat · 15 mg cholesterol · 654 mg sodium · excellent source calcium, iron, vitamin C, folacin

Sweet Potato Celeriac Pie

This is a thoroughly satisfying main course served with a fresh green salad and glass of apple cider. Celeriac has a sweet parsley-like flavour that combines wonderfully with sweet potato, red onion and dill.

Preparation time: 30 minutes

Preheat oven to 400°F (200°C)

Cooking time: 30 minutes

Makes 10 servings (2 pies)

2 tbsp	olive oil	25 mL
2 cups	diced red onion	500 mL
2 cups	diced peeled sweet potato	500 mL
2 cups	diced celeriac	500 mL
1 cup	diced carrot	250 mL
2 cups	vegetable stock (page 49) or water	500 mL
1 tsp	salt	5 mL
2	large eggs	2
1 cup	milk or soy milk	250 mL
¼ cup	chopped fresh dill	50 mL
2 tbsp	almond nut butter	25 mL
¼ tsp	freshly ground black pepper	1 mL
2	unbaked 9-inch (23 cm) pastry shells	2
¾ cup	coarsely chopped roasted tamari almonds (page 13)	175 mL

In large skillet or Dutch oven, heat oil over medium heat. Cook onion for 5 minutes or until softened. Add sweet potato, celeriac and carrot; cook for 2 minutes.

Add stock and salt; cover and simmer for 20 minutes or until vegetables are softened and liquid has evaporated. Transfer, in batches, to food processor fitted with metal blade; purée until smooth.

In large bowl, whisk together eggs, milk, dill, almond butter and pepper. Add vegetable purée, whisking to combine. Divide between pastry shells; sprinkle with almonds. Bake in 400°F (200°C) oven for 30 minutes or until centre is firm.

Per serving: 326 calories · 8 g protein · 20 g total fat · 31 g carbohydrate · 3 g fibre (moderate) · 4 g saturated fat · 45 mg cholesterol · 740 mg sodium

Soba Noodles with Red Onions, Black Beans and Kale

Soba noodles contain buckwheat flour, resemble fragile sticks and cook quickly. Read the label to see what percentage of buckwheat is used. Choose noodles with the most buckwheat. My favourite brand, Sobaya, uses a 60–40 ratio of buckwheat and unbleached white flours.

Preparation time: 30 minutes

Makes 6 servings

2 tbsp	toasted sesame oil	25 mL
2	cloves garlic, minced	2
2	red onions, thinly sliced	2
1 cup	sliced button mushrooms (or assortment)	250 mL
1 tbsp	mirin	15 mL
1 tbsp	ground cumin	15 mL
1 tsp	salt	5 mL
¼ tsp	freshly ground black pepper	1 mL
1	bunch kale (about 1 lb/500 g), rinsed and stemmed	1
1½ cups	cooked black beans	375 mL
1 cup	vegetable stock or water	250 mL
¼ cup	tahini	50 mL
¼ cup	finely chopped fresh coriander	50 mL
1 tbsp	fresh lemon juice	15 mL
8 oz	soba noodles	250 g

In large skillet, heat oil over medium heat. Cook garlic and onions for 5 minutes or until softened. Stir in mushrooms, mirin, cumin, ½ tsp (2 mL) of the salt and pepper; cook for 5 minutes or until very soft.

Meanwhile, bring large pot of salted water to boil. Add kale; cook for 5 minutes. Remove with slotted spoon to strainer; let drain. Add to onions along with beans and vegetable stock; simmer for 5 minutes. Reduce heat; stir in tahini, coriander, lemon juice and remaining salt.

Return reserved water to boil. Add noodles; cook until just tender, about 5 minutes. Drain and toss with kale mixture.

Tip: Instead of cooking your own black beans (see pages 8 to 9), you can use 1 can (14 oz/398 mL), drained and rinsed.

Per serving: 368 calories · 16 g protein · 11 g total fat · 58 g carbohydrate · 7 g fibre (very high) · 2 g saturated fat · 0 mg cholesterol · 589 mg sodium · excellent source iron, vitamin C, folacin

Veggies in a Pita

I discovered this crowd-pleasing luncheon special at a Toronto health food deli that I once owned. Garnish the pockets with sliced tomatoes, sprouts and salsa.

Preparation time: 35 minutes

Preheat oven to 300°F (150°C)

Makes 6 servings

¼ cup	canola oil	50 mL
3	cloves garlic, minced	3
2	red onions, halved and thinly sliced	2
1	portobello mushroom, sliced	1
1	Japanese eggplant, thinly sliced diagonally	1
1	carrot, grated	1
1	sweet red pepper, thinly sliced	1
2	stalks celery, thinly sliced	2
2 tbsp	tamari	25 mL
¼ cup	unbleached white flour	50 mL
1 tbsp	curry powder	15 mL
1 cup	soy milk	250 mL
4 oz	firm tofu, rinsed and puréed	125 g
½ tsp	salt	2 mL
¼ tsp	freshly ground black pepper	1 mL
6	round (4 inch/10 cm) pita breads, halved	6

In large skillet, heat 2 tbsp (25 mL) of the oil over medium heat; cook garlic for 1 minute or until browned. Add onions; cook for 5 minutes or until softened. Add mushroom, eggplant, carrot, red pepper, celery and tamari; cook, stirring often, for 12 minutes or until softened.

Meanwhile, in saucepan, heat remaining oil over medium heat. Whisk in flour and curry powder; cook until lightly browned, about 3 minutes. Whisk in soy milk; bring to boil. Reduce heat and cook, whisking, for 3 minutes or until thickened. Whisk in puréed tofu, salt and pepper; cook until heated through, about 2 minutes. Stir into vegetables; heat through.

Heat pitas in 300°F (150°C) oven for 5 minutes or until warm. Using heaping ½ cup (125 mL) for each, stuff pitas with filling.

Per serving: 373 calories · 12 g protein · 12 g total fat · 56 g carbohydrate · 5 g fibre (high)
· 1 g saturated fat · 0 mg cholesterol · 765 mg sodium
· excellent source iron, vitamin C, folacin · good source calcium

Sun-Dried Tomato Risotto with Garlic and Greens

Risotto is a general term for a creamy northern Italian rice dish made with short-grain white rice. The addition of roasted garlic, sun-dried tomatoes and freshly grated Parmesan cheese turns it into a tasty meal.

Preparation time: 1 hour

Preheat oven to 350°F (180°C)

Makes 4 servings

12	cloves garlic (unpeeled)	12
2 tbsp	olive oil	25 mL
½ cup	dry-packed sun-dried tomatoes	125 mL
2	medium leeks (white and light green parts only), washed and cut into ¼-inch (5 mm) thick slices	2
1 cup	arborio rice	250 mL
½ cup	mirin or dry white wine	125 mL
3 cups	Swiss chard leaves, washed, stemmed and sliced into ¼-inch (5 mm) wide strips	750 mL
¾ cup	freshly grated Parmesan cheese	175 mL
2 tbsp	chopped fresh parsley	25 mL
1 tsp	salt	5 mL

In small baking dish, toss garlic with 1 tbsp (15 mL) of the oil; cover and bake in 350°F (180°C) oven for 30 minutes or until tender. Uncover and bake for about 8 minutes longer or until very tender. Let cool and peel. With fork, mash until puréed.

Meanwhile, in bowl, cover sun-dried tomatoes with 1 cup (250 mL) boiling water; let stand for 20 minutes. Drain and cut into thin slices.

In saucepan, bring 6 cups (1.5 L) water to simmer. Reduce heat to low; cover and keep hot.

In large saucepan, heat remaining oil over medium heat. Add leeks, tomato slices and half of the garlic purée; sauté until leeks are softened, about 5 minutes.

Add rice; cook, stirring constantly, for 3 minutes. Add mirin; stir until absorbed. Add 1 cup (250 mL) of the hot water and adjust heat until liquid is bubbling gently; stir until liquid is absorbed. Continue adding 3 cups (750 mL) of the remaining water, 1 cup (250 mL) at a time, waiting until each is absorbed and stirring frequently before adding next.

Add Swiss chard. Continue adding remaining 2 cups (500 mL) hot water, 1 cup (250 mL) at a time, waiting until each is absorbed and stirring frequently, until rice is just tender, about 20 minutes.

Stir in remaining garlic purée, Parmesan, parsley and salt. Serve immediately.

Per serving: 400 calories · 14 g protein · 13 g total fat · 55 g carbohydrate · 4 g fibre (high) · 5 g saturated fat · 15 mg cholesterol · 1146 mg sodium · excellent source calcium · good source iron

Japanese Eggplant with Miso and Curry Paste

Japanese eggplants are long and slender with a deep purple colour. Since they absorb flavours readily, the spices, wine and curry paste make them unbelievably delicious in this dish. Serve with rice or noodles.

Preparation time: 20 minutes

Makes 4 servings

2 cups	green beans	500 mL
2	Japanese eggplants	2
¼ cup	toasted sesame oil	50 mL
4	green onions, cut into 1-inch (2.5 cm) pieces	4
1	small carrot, grated	1
4	cloves garlic, minced	4
2 tsp	minced fresh gingerroot	10 mL
2 tsp	mellow miso	10 mL
1 tsp	mirin or white wine	5 mL
1 tsp	red curry paste	5 mL
2 tbsp	toasted sesame seeds	25 mL

Trim beans and cut into 1-inch (2.5 cm) pieces; steam for 3 minutes or until just tender. Slice eggplants lengthwise into ½-inch (1 cm) thick slices; cut into ½-inch (1 cm) wide strips and cut again into 3-inch (8 cm) pieces.

In large skillet, heat oil over medium-high heat; cook eggplant until lightly browned, about 3 minutes. Stir in beans, onions and carrot; cook for 2 minutes. Stir in garlic and ginger; cook for 1 minute.

Stir together ¼ cup (50 mL) water, miso, mirin and curry paste; stir into vegetables and toss to coat. Garnish with sesame seeds.

Per serving: 206 calories · 4 g protein · 17 g total fat · 13 g carbohydrate · 4 g fibre (high) · 2 g saturated fat · 0 mg cholesterol · 120 mg sodium · good source folacin

Marinated Gourmet Rice with Veggies

When rice is combined with red onions, artichoke hearts, arame and pine nuts, every mouthful becomes one to remember.

Preparation time: 20 minutes

Marinating time: 1 hour

Makes 6 servings

½ cup	arame	125 mL
2½ cups	cooked brown rice (about 1 cup/250 mL raw)	625 mL
1	carrot, grated	1
2	stalks celery, sliced	2
1	sweet red pepper, thinly sliced	1
Half	red onion, halved lengthwise and thinly sliced	Half
1	jar (7 oz/199 mL) artichoke hearts, drained and quartered	1
¼ cup	finely chopped fresh basil	50 mL
2 tbsp	toasted pine nuts	25 mL
DRESSING:		
⅓ cup	tamari	75 mL
¼ cup	rice vinegar	50 mL
¼ cup	mango or apricot jam	50 mL
1 tbsp	minced fresh gingerroot	15 mL
3	cloves garlic	3
1 tsp	Dijon mustard	5 mL

Soak arame in 1 cup (250 mL) water for 5 minutes; drain. In large bowl, toss together rice, carrot, celery, red pepper, onion, artichoke hearts, arame and basil.

Dressing: In food processor or blender, combine tamari, rice vinegar, jam, ginger, garlic and mustard; process until well blended. Add to rice mixture; toss. Let stand for 1 hour or overnight. Sprinkle with pine nuts.

Per serving: 204 calories · 7 g protein · 3 g total fat · 41 g carbohydrate · 5 g fibre (high)
· trace saturated fat · 0 mg cholesterol · 1076 mg sodium
· excellent source vitamin C · good source iron, folacin

Tri-Colour Peppers Stuffed with Chickpeas, Mint and Pine Nuts

This is my favourite meal to take to a potluck. Just cook the stuffed peppers when you arrive.

Preparation time: 30 minutes

Preheat oven to 350°F (180°C)

Cooking time: 25 minutes

Makes 8 servings

½ cup	millet, rinsed	125 mL
2 tbsp	olive oil	25 mL
1	large onion, finely chopped	1
2	stalks celery, finely chopped	2
2	cloves garlic, minced	2
1	green onion, chopped	1
1	large carrot, grated	1
1 cup	cooked chickpeas	250 mL
½ cup	toasted pine nuts	125 mL
2 tbsp	chopped fresh mint	25 mL
1 tbsp	chopped fresh coriander	15 mL
2 tsp	grated lemon zest	10 mL
½ tsp	salt	2 mL
¼ tsp	freshly ground black pepper	1 mL
8	medium assorted coloured peppers or 4 large	8
DRESSING:		
¼ cup	olive oil	50 mL
3 tbsp	fresh lemon juice	50 mL

In saucepan, bring 1½ cups (375 mL) water to boil. Add millet; cover, reduce heat and simmer until tender, about 17 minutes. Remove from heat; let stand for 5 minutes. Transfer to large bowl; fluff with fork. Let cool.

Meanwhile, in large nonstick skillet, heat oil over medium heat; cook onion, celery, garlic, green onion and carrot for 7 minutes or until softened. Stir into millet along with chickpeas, pine nuts, mint, coriander, lemon zest, salt and pepper.

Trim tops off peppers; remove seeds and ribs. If necessary, trim bottoms of peppers slightly to level. In large pot of boiling water, blanch peppers for 3 minutes. Refresh under cool water; drain.

Stuff each pepper with about ¾ cup (175 mL) millet mixture, about 1½ cups (375 mL) for large. Place on baking sheet; bake in 350°F (180°C) oven for 25 minutes or until heated through.

Dressing: Whisk oil with lemon juice; drizzle evenly over each pepper immediately after removing from oven.

Tip: Use melon baller to remove seeds and ribs from peppers.

Per serving: 273 calories · 7 g protein · 17 g total fat · 28 g carbohydrate · 6 g fibre (very high) · 2 g saturated fat · 0 mg cholesterol · 165 mg sodium · excellent source vitamin C, folacin · good source iron

Basmati Burger Pockets with Coriander Yogurt Sauce

━ ━ ━

The irresistible fragrance of these burgers cooking whets everyone's appetite. Rice is the most widely consumed food in the world and basmati, a long-grain rice grown in India, Pakistan and the Himalayan foothills, is one of the most aromatic.

Preparation time: 45 minutes

Heat broiler to high

Makes 12 servings

1 cup	basmati rice, rinsed	250 mL
2 tbsp	olive oil	25 mL
5	cloves garlic, minced	5
2	large onions, thinly sliced	2
2 cups	button mushrooms, sliced	500 mL
2 tsp	chopped fresh thyme	10 mL
1 tsp	ground cumin	5 mL
3	eggs, lightly beaten	3
2 cups	fresh bread crumbs (about 3 slices)	500 mL
½ tsp	salt	2 mL
¼ tsp	freshly ground black pepper	1 mL
6	whole wheat pita breads	6
12	lettuce leaves	12
5	plum tomatoes, sliced	5
CORIANDER YOGURT SAUCE:		
1	clove garlic, crushed	1
¼ tsp	salt	1 mL
¾ cup	low-fat plain yogurt	175 mL
1 tbsp	chopped fresh coriander	15 mL

In saucepan, bring rinsed rice and 2 cups (500 mL) water to boil. Reduce heat and simmer gently for 15 minutes or until water has been absorbed. Transfer to large bowl. Let cool.

Meanwhile, in large nonstick skillet, heat oil over medium heat. Cook garlic and onions for 5 minutes or until softened. Add mushrooms, thyme and cumin; cook for 7 minutes or until softened.

Stir eggs into rice until well blended. Stir in vegetable mixture, bread crumbs, salt and pepper until thoroughly blended and mixture holds together.

Using heaping ½ cup (125 mL) for each, shape into 12 patties. Place on lightly greased baking sheet; broil, turning once, for 6 minutes or until lightly browned.

Coriander Yogurt Sauce: Meanwhile, with side of knife, mash garlic with salt to form paste. In bowl, stir together garlic, yogurt and coriander.

Meanwhile, warm pitas; halve and open to form pockets. Place burger into each along with 1 tbsp (15 mL) sauce, lettuce leaf and tomato slices.

Per serving: 229 calories · 8 g protein · 5 g total fat · 38 g carbohydrate · 4 g fibre (high) · 1 g saturated fat · 55 mg cholesterol · 385 mg sodium

Curried Parsnip and Bean Burgers

———

I adore tender, sweet parsnips. Combined with chickpeas, they make a tasty base that gets dressed up with even more flavour once the portobello mushrooms, garlic and onions are added. These burgers are delicious hot or cold. Serve in buns.

Preparation time: 35 minutes

Cooking time: 8 minutes

Makes 8 servings

1½ lb	parsnips (about 5), washed, peeled and sliced	750 g
1	can (19 oz/540 mL) chickpeas	1
¼ cup	olive oil	50 mL
2	cloves garlic, minced	2
1	large Spanish onion, diced	1
2	portobello mushrooms, stemmed and chopped	2
1 tbsp	mirin	15 mL
1 tsp	tamari	5 mL
3 tbsp	curry powder	50 mL
½ tsp	salt	2 mL
¼ tsp	cayenne pepper	1 mL
1 cup	dry bread crumbs	250 mL
¼ cup	chopped fresh coriander	50 mL
1 tsp	brown rice vinegar	5 mL

Steam parsnips until tender, about 8 minutes. Mash and set aside.

Drain chickpeas, reserving 3 tbsp (50 mL) liquid; rinse chickpeas and place in food processor fitted with metal blade. Add reserved liquid; purée to make paste. Set aside.

In large skillet, heat 2 tbsp (25 mL) of the oil over medium heat. Cook garlic and onion for 5 minutes or until softened. Add mushrooms, mirin and tamari; cook for 5 minutes or until mushrooms are softened.

Stir in curry powder, salt and cayenne. Stir in parsnips and chickpeas; mix well. Stir in ½ cup (125 mL) of the bread crumbs, coriander and vinegar; mix well.

Using heaping ½ cup (125 mL) for each, form into eight 4-inch (10 cm) patties. In shallow bowl, coat patties with remaining bread crumbs.

In large skillet, heat remaining oil over medium-high heat. Cook patties, turning once, for 8 minutes or until browned.

Tip: Instead of frying the burgers, you can bake them on a nonstick baking sheet in 350°F (180°C) oven, turning once, for 15 minutes.

Per burger: 273 calories · 7 g protein · 9 g total fat · 43 g carbohydrate · 6 g fibre (very high)
· 1 g saturated fat · 0 mg cholesterol · 418 mg sodium
· excellent source folacin · good source iron

Cheesy Vegetable Bean Burritos

Lime juice, sun-dried tomatoes, coriander and shiitake mushrooms add
sunny fresh flavour to popular burrito wrap-ups.

Preparation time: 35 minutes

Makes 8 servings

½ cup	dry-packed sun-dried tomatoes	125 mL
½ cup	arame	125 mL
2 tbsp	olive oil	25 mL
1	red onion, sliced	1
3	cloves garlic, minced	3
1	sweet red pepper, chopped	1
1 cup	sliced shiitake mushrooms	250 mL
1	zucchini, halved lengthwise and sliced	1
¼ cup	chopped fresh coriander	50 mL
1 tbsp	fresh lime juice	15 mL
1 tbsp	chili powder	15 mL
1 tsp	each ground cumin and dried oregano	5 mL
1	can (14 oz/398 mL) black beans, drained and rinsed	1
1 cup	corn kernels	250 mL
8	10-inch (25 cm) flour tortillas	8
1 cup	shredded Monterey Jack cheese	250 mL

Cover tomatoes with 1 cup (250mL) boiling water; let stand for 10 minutes. Drain and chop finely. Meanwhile, soak arame in 1 cup (250 mL)
cold water for 5 minutes; drain.

Meanwhile, in large skillet, heat oil over medium heat. Cook red
onion and garlic for 5 minutes or until softened. Add drained arame, red
pepper, mushrooms and zucchini; cook for 5 minutes.

Add chopped tomatoes, coriander, lime juice, chili powder, cumin and oregano; cook for 3 minutes. Stir in beans and corn; cook, stirring, until heated through, about 3 minutes.

In another skillet, warm tortillas over medium heat for 2 minutes, turning once. Place heaping ½ cup (125 mL) filling down centre of each, leaving 1-inch (2.5 cm) border at bottom and top. Sprinkle each with 2 tbsp (25 mL) cheese. Fold bottom edge over filling; fold sides over. Roll up from the bottom.

Per serving: 379 calories · 14 g protein · 12 g total fat · 55 g carbohydrate · 7 g fibre (very high)
· 4 g saturated fat · 13 mg cholesterol · 583 mg sodium
· excellent source iron, vitamin C, folacin · good source calcium

Great Northern Bean Cakes

My mother, Helen, has been cooking Great Northern beans for 50 years. She never buys canned white cannellini beans, but I do. Generously spiced, the beans make a burger that has a pleasing texture and taste. Serve with Mango Kiwi Salsa (page 46).

Preparation time: 20 minutes

Makes 4 servings

2	cans (14 oz/398 mL each) Great Northern or cannellini beans, drained	2
½ cup	finely chopped red onion	125 mL
¼ cup	chopped fresh dill	50 mL
1	egg white	1
½ cup	dry bread crumbs	125 mL
2	cloves garlic, minced	2
1 tsp	ground cumin	5 mL
½ tsp	ground allspice	2 mL
Pinch	cayenne pepper	Pinch
¼ tsp	each salt and freshly ground black pepper	1 mL
2 tbsp	olive oil	25 mL

Place beans in large bowl and coarsely mash. Stir in onion, dill, egg white, 2 tbsp (25 mL) of the bread crumbs, garlic, cumin, allspice, cayenne, salt and pepper.

Place remaining bread crumbs in shallow pan. Using ¼ cup (50 mL) bean mixture for each burger, form into eight ¼-inch (5 mm) thick cakes. Coat both sides with bread crumbs.

In skillet, heat oil over medium heat; cook bean cakes, turning once, for 8 minutes or until golden brown.

Per serving of 2 cakes: 302 calories · 14 g protein · 8 g total fat · 44 g carbohydrate · 9 g fibre (very high) · 1 g saturated fat · 0 mg cholesterol · 265 mg sodium · excellent source folacin · good source iron

Black Bean Quinoa Burgers

This is my all-time favourite veggie burger. Rinse the quinoa for 5 minutes in a fine-meshed sieve to remove the bitter taste. Get the hamburger buns ready and serve these with salsa or sour cream boosted with lime zest and juice.

Preparation time: 25 minutes

Makes 6 burgers

1 cup	quinoa, rinsed	250 mL
1	can (14 oz/398 mL) black beans, drained and rinsed	1
½ cup	grated red onion, squeezed dry	125 mL
¼ cup	chopped fresh coriander	50 mL
3 tbsp	extra virgin olive oil	50 mL
2	cloves garlic, minced	2
Half	jalapeño pepper, seeded and chopped	Half
¾ tsp	salt	4 mL
½ tsp	each chili powder and ground cumin	2 mL
¼ tsp	freshly ground black pepper	1 mL
⅓ cup	coarse dry bread crumbs	75 mL

In saucepan, bring 1½ cups (375 mL) water to boil; add quinoa and return to boil. Reduce heat and simmer for 15 minutes or until water has been absorbed.

Transfer to food processor fitted with metal blade. Add beans, onion, coriander, 1 tbsp (15 mL) of the oil, garlic, jalapeño, salt, chili powder, cumin and pepper; purée until smooth.

Using ½ cup (125 mL) for each, form into six ½-inch (1 cm) thick patties. Place bread crumbs in shallow bowl. Press patties into crumbs, turning to coat both sides.

In nonstick skillet, heat remaining oil over medium-high heat. Cook patties, in batches and turning once, for 8 minutes or until browned.

Per serving: 258 calories · 9 g protein · 9 g total fat · 37 g carbohydrate · 5 g fibre (high) · 1 g saturated fat · 0 mg cholesterol · 450 mg sodium · excellent source iron, folacin

Lentil Pistachio Loaf

My husband, Jim, likes a slice of this loaf on toasted Russian rye bread.

Preparation time: 30 minutes

Preheat oven to 350°F (180°C)

Cooking time: 1 hour

Makes 4 servings

1 cup	dried lentils	250 mL
1 cup	apple cider	250 mL
2 tbsp	butter	25 mL
¼ cup	dry bread crumbs	50 mL
1	onion, grated	1
2	cloves garlic, minced	2
1	carrot, grated	1
1	stalk celery, chopped	1
½ cup	coarsely ground pistachios	125 mL
½ cup	grated old Cheddar cheese	125 mL
2 tbsp	chopped fresh parsley	25 mL
1 tbsp	each chopped fresh sage and thyme	15 mL
3	eggs, lightly beaten	3
½ tsp	each salt and freshly ground black pepper	2 mL

In saucepan, bring 1 cup (250 mL) water, lentils and cider to boil; reduce heat, partially cover and simmer for 20 minutes or until lentils are tender and liquid has been absorbed.

Meanwhile, line 8- x 4-inch (1.5 L) loaf pan with parchment paper. Brush with 1 tbsp (15 mL) of the butter; coat with 1 tbsp (15 mL) of the bread crumbs.

In skillet, heat remaining butter over medium heat. Cook onion, garlic, carrot and celery for 8 minutes or until softened. Mix in lentils, pistachios, Cheddar, parsley, sage, thyme, eggs, salt and pepper. Spoon into prepared pan, packing down to form smooth surface.

Cover with foil; bake in 350°F (180°C) oven for 50 minutes. Uncover and bake for 10 minutes longer or until browned. Run knife around edges and turn out onto serving dish.

Per serving: 466 calories · 25 g protein · 20 g total fat · 50 g carbohydrate · 8 g fibre (very high) · 9 g saturated fat · 192 mg cholesterol · 559 mg sodium · excellent source iron, folacin · good source calcium

Bean and Pepper Pie

When my daughter, Mackenzie, was in nursery school, she learned to sing *Can You Bake a Cherry Pie?* One day when she arrived home, I had all the ingredients ready for this filling bean pie and a new song was born. Use soy yogurt and bread crumbs instead of the plain yogurt and Cheddar cheese for a dairy-free dish. You can also use 3 cups (750 mL) canned, drained and rinsed beans in place of dried beans.

Preparation time: 1½ hours

Preheat oven to 350°F (180°C)

Cooking time: 20 minutes

Makes 8 servings

1¼ cups	whole wheat pastry flour	300 mL
1 tsp	each ground cumin and chili powder	5 mL
½ tsp	each paprika and salt	2 mL
½ cup	cold butter, cut into pieces	125 mL
2 tbsp	ice water	25 mL
	FILLING:	
1 cup	dried black beans, rinsed and soaked	250 mL
1	bay leaf	1
1	red onion, halved	1
1 cup	plain yogurt	250 mL
½ tsp	salt	2 mL
¼ tsp	freshly ground black pepper	1 mL
1 cup	corn kernels	250 mL
1	each sweet red and green pepper, chopped	1
¾ cup	grated Cheddar cheese	175 mL
½ cup	good-tasting nutritional yeast	125 mL
1	jalapeño pepper, seeded and finely chopped	1
½ cup	chopped green onions (about 6)	125 mL
¼ cup	chopped fresh coriander	50 mL

In food processor fitted with metal blade, blend together flour, cumin, chili powder, paprika and salt. Add butter; blend until mixture resembles coarse meal. Add ice water; pulse until mixture forms ball.

With floured hands, press dough evenly onto bottom and halfway up side of 9-inch (2.5 L) springform pan. Chill for 10 minutes. Bake in 350°F (180°C) oven for 15 minutes; let cool. (Crust can be covered and set aside at room temperature for up to 1 day.)

Filling: In bowl, soak beans in 5 cups (1.25 L) water for 6 hours. Drain and rinse. In large pot, bring beans, 2½ cups (625 mL) water, bay leaf and onion to boil; reduce heat and simmer, uncovered, for 1¼ hours or until tender. Drain, discarding bay leaf and onion.

In food processor fitted with metal blade, purée together 2 cups (500 mL) of the beans, yogurt, salt and pepper. Spread evenly onto crust.

In large bowl, stir together corn, red and green peppers, cheese, yeast, jalapeño, green onions, coriander and remaining beans; spread over bean mixture, pressing down gently. Bake in 350°F (180°C) oven for 20 minutes. Let cool for 10 minutes. Serve hot or at room temperature.

Per serving: 416 calories · 20 g protein · 18 g total fat · 50 g carbohydrate · 10 g fibre (very high)
· 10 g saturated fat · 44 mg cholesterol · 513 mg sodium
· excellent source iron, vitamin C, folacin · good source calcium

Quinoa Chili

━━ ━━ ━━

This is the best kid-friendly chili in the world. At a winter solstice party last year, five-year-old Jacob Barrett had a spoonful of this on his plate. His mother, Tammy, and I watched with delight as he heaped his plate with more and ate it all.

Preparation time: 40 minutes

Makes 8 servings

1 cup	quinoa, rinsed and patted dry	250 mL
¼ tsp	salt	1 mL
2 tbsp	canola oil	25 mL
1	onion, chopped	1
3	cloves garlic, minced	3
1	sweet green pepper, chopped	1
2	Japanese eggplants, chopped (about 2 cups/500 mL)	2
2	stalks celery, chopped	2
1 tbsp	each chili powder and dried oregano	15 mL
1 tsp	Hungarian paprika	5 mL
½ tsp	each salt and freshly ground black pepper	2 mL
2	cans (28 oz/796 mL each) diced tomatoes	2
1 tbsp	packed brown sugar	15 mL
2	green onions, sliced	2
1	small bunch broccoli, cut into florets and blanched	1

In skillet over medium heat, roast quinoa for 5 minutes or until fragrant and beginning to pop. In small saucepan, bring 2 cups (500 mL) water and salt to boil. Add roasted quinoa; cover and simmer over medium heat for 15 to 20 minutes or until water has been absorbed. Remove from heat and stir; let stand, covered, for 10 minutes.

Meanwhile, in large saucepan, heat oil over medium heat. Cook onion and garlic for 5 minutes or until softened. Stir in green pepper, eggplants, celery, chili powder, oregano, paprika, salt and pepper; cook for 10 minutes, stirring often.

Stir in tomatoes and sugar; simmer for 15 to 20 minutes or until thickened, stirring occasionally. Stir in quinoa, green onions and broccoli; cook until just heated through.

Per serving: 192 calories · 7 g protein · 6 g total fat · 32 g carbohydrate · 6 g fibre (very high)
· 1 g saturated fat · 0 mg cholesterol · 580 mg sodium
· excellent source iron, vitamin C · good source folacin

Stir-Fried Tofu with Vegetables in Curried Almond Butter Sauce

━━ ━━ ━━

One evening when my daughter, Mackenzie, was about three years old, she refused to eat her dinner. It was this old family standard, but my husband, Jim, had added some leftover spinach at the last minute and turned the mixture green! Nevertheless, this version has become a favourite.

Preparation time: 25 minutes

Makes 4 servings

¼ cup	almond nut butter	50 mL
3 tbsp	tamari	50 mL
2 tbsp	mirin	25 mL
2 tbsp	toasted sesame oil	25 mL
1 tbsp	curry powder	15 mL
	STIR-FRY:	
2 tbsp	olive oil	25 mL
12 oz	firm tofu, rinsed and cut into ½-inch (1 cm) cubes	375 g
3	cloves garlic, minced	3
½ tsp	dried rosemary	2 mL
1	red onion, thinly sliced	1
1	sweet red pepper, thinly sliced	1
1	carrot, grated	1
2	stalks broccoli (florets and stalks), sliced	2
1 tbsp	tamari	15 mL
Half	bunch fresh spinach, washed and stemmed	Half

In bowl, whisk together almond butter, tamari, mirin, sesame oil and curry powder. Set aside.

Stir-Fry: In large wok, heat oil over high heat; stir-fry tofu for about 10 minutes or until golden. Transfer tofu to sauce; stir to coat. Set aside.

Add garlic, rosemary and onion to wok; stir-fry for about 5 minutes or until onions are browned. Stir in red pepper, carrot, broccoli, tamari and 2 tbsp (25 mL) water; cover and cook until vegetables are tender, about 5 minutes.

Add spinach and tofu with sauce; cook for 2 minutes or until spinach is wilted and tofu is heated through.

Per serving: 394 calories · 16 g protein · 27 g total fat · 27 g carbohydrate · 6 g fibre (very high)
· 3 g saturated fat · 0 mg cholesterol · 1075 mg sodium
· excellent source calcium, iron, vitamin C, folacin

Tofu Nuggets with Swiss Chard

One day my kids came home from school upset that they couldn't have the same fast food chicken nuggets that their friends were eating. So I promised to make vegetarian nuggets that would be just as cool.

Preparation time: 20 minutes

Makes 4 servings

1 lb	firm tofu, rinsed and pressed	500 g
¼ cup	smooth almond nut butter	50 mL
2 tbsp	Dijon mustard	25 mL
2 tbsp	fresh lemon juice	25 mL
2 tbsp	liquid honey	25 mL
¼ tsp	salt	1 mL
¼ cup	sesame seeds	50 mL
¼ cup	toasted sesame oil	50 mL
6 cups	coarsely chopped stemmed rinsed Swiss chard	1.5 L
6	cloves garlic, minced	6
1 tbsp	minced fresh gingerroot	15 mL
2 tbsp	soy sauce	25 mL

Cut tofu into ½- x ¼-inch (1 cm x 5 mm) cubes. In bowl, whisk together almond butter, mustard, lemon juice, honey and salt; add tofu and toss to coat. With slotted spoon, remove to shallow dish, reserving remaining sauce. Sprinkle with sesame seeds to coat.

In large nonstick skillet, heat 3 tbsp (50 mL) of the sesame oil over medium-high heat. Cook tofu, turning until browned on all sides, about 7 minutes. Remove and keep warm.

Add remaining oil to skillet; cook Swiss chard over medium heat for 3 minutes. Add garlic and ginger; cook for 3 minutes. Stir in soy sauce. Place on platter; pile tofu on top. Drizzle with reserved sauce.

Per serving: 425 calories · 17 g protein · 34 g total fat · 20 g carbohydrate · 3 g fibre (moderate) · 4 g saturated fat · 0 mg cholesterol · 866 mg sodium · excellent source iron · good source calcium, folacin

Tofu with Leeks and Peanut Butter

—— —— ——

Honey, vinegar and ginger flavour tofu with a sweet yet piquant taste that complements the mellow leeks. Members of the onion family, leeks are usually quite sandy and need a thorough rinse. Always trim off and discard the root end.

Preparation time: 20 minutes

Makes 4 servings

½ cup	arame	125 mL
3 tbsp	toasted sesame oil	50 mL
2	leeks (white part only), rinsed and sliced	2
1	each sweet red and green pepper, sliced	1
1	carrot, grated	1
1 tsp	minced fresh gingerroot	5 mL
3 tbsp	peanut butter	50 mL
2 tbsp	liquid honey	25 mL
1 tbsp	red wine vinegar	15 mL
2 tsp	tamari	10 mL
¼ tsp	cayenne pepper	1 mL
1 lb	firm tofu, rinsed, pressed and cut into 1-inch (2.5 cm) cubes	500 g

Soak arame in 1 cup (250 mL) cold water for 5 minutes; drain.

Meanwhile, in wok or large skillet, heat 2 tbsp (25 mL) of the sesame oil over medium-high heat. Stir-fry leeks and red and green peppers for 3 minutes. Add carrot and ginger; stir-fry for 2 minutes. Arrange arame in layer to cover vegetables. Cover and remove from heat.

In medium bowl, whisk together remaining sesame oil, peanut butter, honey, vinegar, tamari and cayenne pepper; add tofu and toss to coat. Add to vegetables and return to heat. Stir-fry for 3 minutes or until heated through.

Per serving: 455 calories · 18 g protein · 23 g total fat · 53 g carbohydrate · 8 g fibre (very high)
· 3 g saturated fat · 0 mg cholesterol · 1402 mg sodium
· excellent source calcium, iron, vitamin C, folacin

Tofu Lasagna

——— ——— ———

We can talk about what an excellent source of digestible protein it is, but many of us find tofu lacking in flavour. My solution is to team it up with fabulous flavours. In this recipe the tofu is infused with the flavour of a delicious tomato sauce seasoned with wine, garlic and fresh basil. A true East meets West meal!

Preparation time: 1 hour

Preheat oven to 375°F (190°C)

Cooking time: 45 minutes

Makes 8 servings

3	sheets (13 x 9-inch/33 x 23 cm) fresh lasagna noodles or 9 cooked dried lasagna noodles	3
8 oz	shredded mozzarella cheese	250 g
3 tbsp	freshly grated Parmesan cheese	50 mL
	TOMATO SAUCE:	
3 tbsp	olive oil	50 mL
1	medium onion, chopped	1
1 tbsp	minced garlic	15 mL
1	sweet green pepper, chopped	1
1	can (28 oz/796 mL) crushed tomatoes	1
1	can (5½ oz/156 mL) tomato paste	1
2 tbsp	dry red wine or mirin	25 mL
2 tsp	tamari	10 mL
1 tsp	dried oregano	5 mL
¼ tsp	freshly ground black pepper	1 mL
2	bay leaves	2
½ cup	chopped fresh basil	125 mL
	FILLING:	
2 cups	ricotta cheese	500 mL
8 oz	firm tofu, rinsed and puréed	250 g
1 tsp	tamari	5 mL
¼ tsp	freshly ground black pepper	1 mL

Tomato Sauce: In large saucepan, heat oil over medium heat. Cook onion and garlic for about 5 minutes or until softened. Add green pepper, tomatoes, tomato paste, red wine, tamari, oregano, pepper and bay leaves; reduce heat and simmer, covered and stirring occasionally, for 40 minutes. Discard bay leaves. Stir in basil. Set aside.

Filling: In bowl, mix together ricotta, tofu, tamari and pepper; set aside.

Spread a little sauce over bottom of 13- x 9-inch (3 L) baking dish. Cover with layer of noodles. Spread with half of the filling. Cover with one-third of the sauce. Sprinkle with half of the mozzarella. Cover with another layer of noodles. Repeat layers once. Cover with remaining sauce.

Sprinkle Parmesan evenly over top. Cover and bake in 375°F (190°C) oven for 25 minutes. Uncover and bake for 10 minutes. Let stand for 10 minutes before serving.

Per serving: 444 calories · 23 g protein · 23 g total fat · 39 g carbohydrate · 5 g fibre (high)
· 11 g saturated fat · 58 mg cholesterol · 493 mg sodium
· excellent source calcium, vitamin C · good source iron, folacin

Tofu Turkey with Stuffing, Mushroom Gravy and Cranberry Sauce

---

This is the recipe you've been waiting for. All the frills are here: mushroom gravy, cranberry sauce and herb dressing. It takes just about as long to prepare and bake as a regular turkey would. The tofu needs to be basted regularly so that it develops a golden crust.

Preparation time: 1½ hours

Preheat oven to 400°F (200°C)

Cooking time: 1½ hours

Makes 14 servings

	TOFU TURKEY:	
5 lb	firm tofu, rinsed	2.2 kg
3 tbsp	dried sage	50 mL
2 tbsp	each dried marjoram, thyme and rosemary	25 mL
1 tbsp	crushed celery seed	15 mL
1 tbsp	freshly ground black pepper	15 mL
	STUFFING:	
3 tbsp	toasted sesame oil	50 mL
2 cups	thinly sliced washed leeks	500 mL
5	cloves garlic, minced	5
1 tsp	minced fresh gingerroot	5 mL
2	stalks celery, sliced	2
2	portobello mushrooms, chopped	2
1 cup	corn kernels	250 mL
½ cup	tamari	125 mL
5 cups	cubed (½ inch/1 cm) whole wheat bread	1.25 L
½ cup	chopped fresh herbs (parsley, basil and thyme)	125 mL
	BASTING LIQUID:	
¼ cup	toasted sesame oil	50 mL
2 tbsp	tamari	25 mL

MUSHROOM GRAVY:		
2 tbsp	toasted sesame oil	25 mL
1	red onion, chopped	1
6 cups	sliced assorted mushrooms (about 1 lb/500 g)	1.5 L
2 tbsp	white miso	25 mL
½ cup	whole wheat flour	125 mL
1 cup	dry white wine	250 mL
¼ cup	tamari	50 mL
CRANBERRY SAUCE:		
2 cups	cranberries	500 mL
1½ cups	apple juice	375 mL
⅓ cup	maple syrup	75 mL
½ cup	agar-agar flakes	125 mL
¼ tsp	salt	1 mL

Tofu Turkey: Line large colander with single layer of moistened cheesecloth large enough to overhang edge. In food processor, purée tofu; transfer to colander and press to flatten. Fold cheesecloth overhang over top. Place small chopping board on tofu; weigh down with heavy object (such as base of food processor). Let stand for 1 hour to drain liquid from tofu.

Meanwhile, in small bowl, stir together sage, marjoram, thyme, rosemary, celery seed and pepper. Set herb mixture aside.

Stuffing: In large skillet, heat oil over medium heat; cook leeks for 5 minutes. Add garlic, ginger, celery and mushrooms; cook for 5 minutes. Stir in corn, 2 tbsp (25 mL) of the herb mixture and tamari. Reduce heat to low; cover and cook for 5 minutes or until vegetables are softened. Stir in bread cubes and fresh herb mixture; toss until moistened.

Line large shallow bowl (11 inch/28 cm in diameter and 8 cups/4 L volume) with plastic wrap. Remove weight and board from tofu. Stir in

continued

remaining herb mixture. Pack two-thirds into bowl, spreading to 1-inch (2.5 cm) thickness on bottom and side of bowl. Press stuffing into cavity. Cover with remaining tofu, spreading to cover stuffing. Discard cheesecloth. Press down well all over surface. Lightly grease large rimmed baking sheet. Turn tofu out onto sheet, flat side down. Remove plastic wrap.

Basting Liquid: Whisk together sesame oil and tamari. Using brush, lightly baste tofu turkey. Cover with foil and bake in 400°F (200°C) oven for 1 hour. Remove foil; baste and return to oven. Bake, uncovered and basting every 10 minutes, for 30 minutes or until "skin" is golden brown.

Mushroom Gravy: Meanwhile, in large skillet, heat oil over medium-high heat. Cook onion and mushrooms for 7 minutes or until moisture has evaporated and mushrooms turn golden. Stir in miso. Sprinkle with flour; cook for 3 minutes or until flour has been absorbed. Whisk in 2 cups (500 mL) water, wine and tamari; bring to boil, whisking. Reduce heat and simmer, stirring occasionally, for 10 minutes or until thickened.

Cranberry Sauce: In small saucepan, combine cranberries, apple juice, maple syrup, agar-agar and salt; bring to boil over high heat, stirring. Reduce heat and simmer until agar-agar dissolves, about 7 minutes. Transfer to food processor; pulse until chunky. Transfer to serving bowl; cover and let cool to room temperature.

Using two spatulas, transfer tofu turkey to serving platter. Using serrated knife, cut in half lengthwise. Cut into ½-inch (1 cm) thick slices. Serve with gravy and cranberry sauce.

Per serving: 350 calories · 19 g protein · 18 g total fat · 33 g carbohydrate · 5 g fibre (high) · 3 g saturated fat · 0 mg cholesterol · 1224 mg sodium · excellent source calcium, iron, folacin

Orange Garlic Miso Tempeh

Here's something to prepare on the weekend to reheat and serve with noodles, rice or as a sandwich later in the week when time is at a premium.

Preparation time: 25 minutes

Makes 2 servings

2 tbsp	toasted sesame oil	25 mL
5	cloves garlic, minced	5
1 tbsp	minced fresh gingerroot	15 mL
1 tsp	barley miso	5 mL
1 cup	fresh orange juice	250 mL
2 tbsp	mirin	25 mL
1 tbsp	rice vinegar	15 mL
1	pkg (8 oz/250 g) tempeh, quartered	1

In skillet, heat oil over medium heat. Cook garlic and ginger for 2 minutes, stirring.

Whisk miso into orange juice; pour into skillet along with mirin and rice vinegar. Simmer for 3 minutes, stirring.

Add tempeh; cover and simmer over low heat for 16 minutes, turning once. Cut into cubes to serve.

Per serving: 445 calories · 24 g protein · 23 g total fat · 39 g carbohydrate · 1 g fibre · 3 g saturated fat · 0 mg cholesterol · 326 mg sodium · excellent source vitamin C, folacin · good source iron

Tempeh Cabbage Rolls

═══ ═══ ═══

The challenge for this recipe was to duplicate a friend's cabbage rolls without the meat but with just as much flavour. Tempeh marinated in barbecue sauce then mixed with veggies, nuts and berries strikes just the right balance of flavour and texture for delicious results.

Preparation time: 45 minutes

Preheat oven to 350°F (180°C)

Cooking time: 30 minutes

Makes 6 servings

1 cup	Barbecue Sauce (page 187)	250 mL
1 lb	tempeh, cut into ¼-inch (5 mm) cubes	500 g
¼ cup	hijiki	50 mL
2 tbsp	canola oil	25 mL
3	cloves garlic, minced	3
2	onions, thinly sliced	2
1 cup	sliced mushrooms	250 mL
2	stalks celery, thinly sliced	2
2	carrots, grated	2
1 cup	finely sliced cabbage	250 mL
2 cups	cooked basmati rice	500 mL
½ cup	toasted pine nuts	125 mL
½ cup	dried cranberries	125 mL
¼ tsp	each salt and freshly ground black pepper	1 mL
10	green cabbage leaves, cooked	10

In large bowl, pour ½ cup (125 mL) of the Barbecue Sauce over tempeh; toss to coat. Let stand for 15 minutes. Turn tempeh out onto parchment paper-lined baking sheet; bake in 350°F (180°C) oven for 8 minutes.

Meanwhile, soak hijiki in ½ cup (125 mL) cold water for 5 minutes; drain.

In wok or large skillet, heat oil over medium heat. Cook garlic and onions for 5 minutes or until softened. Add mushrooms, celery, carrots, cabbage and hijiki; cook, stirring, for 7 minutes or until softened and liquid has evaporated. Stir in tempeh, rice, pine nuts, cranberries, salt and pepper.

Cut thick vein out of each cabbage leaf. Place ¾ cup (175 mL) tempeh mixture at stem end of each leaf. Roll up envelope style. Place in 13- x 9-inch (3 L) baking dish; pour remaining Barbecue Sauce over top. Bake in 350°F (180°C) oven for 30 minutes or until heated through.

Tip: To cook cabbage leaves, plunge head of cabbage into boiling water and boil for 5 minutes. Lift out of water and cool slightly. Peel off leaves as needed.

Per serving: 539 calories · 23 g protein · 23 g total fat · 68 g carbohydrate · 7 g fibre (very high) · 3 g saturated fat · 0 mg cholesterol · 630 mg sodium · excellent source iron, folacin · good source calcium, vitamin C

Swiss Chard Rolls with Tempeh Filling

My vegetarian friend Eve Weinberg is married to a meat-eating guy. But he is prepared to eat more vegetarian if she can approximate the texture of meat. Here, steamed tempeh spiced up with flavour resembles ground beef. A perfect dish to please everyone.

Preparation time: 45 minutes

Preheat oven to 350°F (180°C)

Cooking time: 30 minutes

Makes 4 servings

2 tbsp	olive oil	25 mL
1	onion, sliced	1
2	cloves garlic, minced	2
1½ cups	assorted sliced mushrooms (button, shiitake, portobello)	375 mL
1	sweet red pepper, chopped	1
2 cups	crushed tomatoes	500 mL
¼ cup	chopped fresh basil	50 mL
2 tsp	packed brown sugar	10 mL
1 tsp	soy sauce	5 mL
¼ tsp	dried rosemary	1 mL
Pinch	cayenne pepper	Pinch
FILLING:		
12 oz	tempeh, cut into 6 squares	375 g
½ cup	finely chopped green onions	125 mL
1	clove garlic, minced	1
2 tbsp	chopped fresh basil	25 mL
1 tsp	Dijon mustard	5 mL
½ tsp	dried thyme	2 mL
Pinch	cayenne pepper	Pinch
2 tbsp	each soy sauce and red wine vinegar	25 mL
1 tbsp	liquid honey	15 mL
1 tsp	hot pepper sauce	5 mL
12	large Swiss chard leaves, rinsed and stemmed	12
¼ cup	freshly grated Parmesan cheese	50 mL

Tomato Sauce: In large skillet, heat oil over medium heat; cook onion and garlic for 5 minutes or until softened. Add mushrooms and red pepper; cook for 3 minutes. Add tomatoes, basil, sugar, soy sauce, rosemary and cayenne; reduce heat and simmer, stirring often, for 20 minutes or until reduced to about 3 cups (750 mL). Set aside.

Filling: Steam tempeh for 10 minutes. In bowl, mash tempeh; stir in green onions, garlic, basil, mustard, thyme and cayenne. Set aside.

In small saucepan, combine soy sauce, vinegar, honey and hot pepper sauce; cook over medium heat until heated through. Stir into tempeh mixture.

Assembling: Steam Swiss chard leaves for about 4 minutes or until just soft and pliable; let cool.

Place 3 tbsp (50 mL) filling at narrow bottom of each leaf. Fold sides over filling and roll up burrito-style. Place rolls, seam side down, in lightly greased 13- x 9-inch (3 L) baking dish; pour tomato sauce over top. Sprinkle with Parmesan. (Rolls can be prepared to this point, covered and refrigerated for up to 8 hours.) Cover with foil. Bake in 350°F (180°C) oven for 30 minutes or until heated through.

Per serving: 372 calories · 24 g protein · 16 g total fat · 41 g carbohydrate · 5 g fibre (high)
· 3 g saturated fat · 5 mg cholesterol · 1010 mg sodium
· excellent source calcium, iron, vitamin C, folacin

Tempeh Kebabs

Good recipes for tempeh tend to tame its fermented flavour. Pungent ingredients such as ginger, garlic, curry, tamarind, soy sauces and citrus juices lend themselves well for this purpose. Serve these kebabs with rice and any remaining marinade. Leftovers can be used to stuff a pita or tossed with noodles. You'll need 10 wooden skewers; be sure to soak them in water for 1 hour before using to prevent scorching.

Preparation time: 50 minutes
Heat grill to medium-high
Cooking time: 8 minutes
Makes 10 kebabs

½ cup	mango juice	125 mL
¼ cup	soy sauce	50 mL
2 tbsp	fresh lemon juice	25 mL
1 tbsp	minced fresh gingerroot	15 mL
4	cloves garlic, thinly sliced	4
2	crushed bay leaves	2
1 tsp	chili powder	5 mL
8 oz	tempeh, cut into 20 cubes	250 g
¼ cup	toasted sesame oil	50 mL
2 tbsp	chopped fresh dill	25 mL
½ tsp	salt	2 mL
Pinch	freshly ground black pepper	Pinch
10	cherry tomatoes, stemmed	10
1	each sweet red and green pepper, cubed	1
1	zucchini, halved lengthwise and cubed	1
10	mushrooms	10
1	red onion, cubed	1

In saucepan, combine mango juice, soy sauce, lemon juice, ginger, garlic, bay leaves and chili powder. Add tempeh and bring to boil. Reduce heat, cover and simmer for 20 minutes. Let cool.

In large bowl, whisk together oil, dill, salt and pepper. Add tomatoes, red and green peppers, zucchini, mushrooms and onion; toss to coat.

Remove tempeh with slotted spoon, reserving marinade. Thread tempeh and vegetables evenly onto 10 soaked wooden skewers, alternating colours.

Cook kebabs, covered, on greased grill, or on baking sheet under broiler, for 8 minutes, turning once and brushing with marinade.

Per kebab: 133 calories · 6 g protein · 7 g total fat · 13 g carbohydrate · 1 g fibre
· 1 g saturated fat · 0 mg cholesterol · 381 mg sodium
· excellent source vitamin C

Tamarind Tempeh Buckwheat Loaf

My cousin Suzie asked me to invent a recipe that looks like meatloaf but isn't. In her family, two members want to eat meat, two don't and she is often stuck trying to please everyone. This mixture of mushroom, eggplant, buckwheat and tamarind provides a filling, delicious combo that satisfies all tastes.

Preparation time: 30 minutes

Preheat oven to 350°F (180°C)

Cooking time: 35 minutes

Makes 8 servings

1 cup	buckwheat groats	250 mL
1 tsp	salt	5 mL
2 tbsp	olive oil	25 mL
3	cloves garlic, minced	3
2	portobello mushrooms, diced	2
1	Japanese eggplant, cut in ½-inch (1 cm) cubes	1
8 oz	tempeh, crumbled	250 g
½ cup	mirin	125 mL
1	sweet red pepper, chopped	1
1 tbsp	tamari	15 mL
¼ cup	tamarind paste	50 mL
¼ cup	chopped fresh coriander	50 mL
½ tsp	cayenne pepper	2 mL
½ tsp	freshly ground black pepper	2 mL
2	eggs, lightly beaten	2
2 tbsp	bread crumbs	25 mL
2 tbsp	good-tasting nutritional yeast	25 mL

In dry heavy skillet, toast buckwheat over medium heat for 5 minutes, stirring. Add 2 cups (500 mL) water and salt; cover and cook over low heat until water is absorbed and buckwheat is tender, about 10 minutes.

Meanwhile, in another large skillet, heat oil over medium heat; cook garlic until lightly browned, about 3 minutes. Add mushrooms; cook for 5 minutes or until softened. Add eggplant, tempeh, mirin, red pepper and tamari; bring to boil, stirring often, for 3 minutes until liquid has been absorbed.

Stir in tamarind paste, coriander, cayenne and pepper; reduce heat and simmer for 3 minutes. In large bowl, stir together eggs, buckwheat and vegetable mixture.

Press mixture firmly into well-greased 9- x 5-inch (2 L) loaf pan. Sprinkle with bread crumbs and yeast. Bake in 350°F (180°C) oven for 35 minutes until firm and crust is browned. Let cool before turning out and cutting with serrated knife to serve.

Per serving: 233 calories · 12 g protein · 8 g total fat · 32 g carbohydrate · 2 g fibre (moderate) · 1 g saturated fat · 54 mg cholesterol · 452 mg sodium · good source iron, vitamin C, folacin

Baked Tempeh and Rice Noodle Salad with Hot Sauce

―― ―― ――

Tempeh does not have to be fried. You can bake it with a marinade and it will absorb the flavour and remain crisp. For a hotter version, add more hot pepper sauce. Perfect for entertaining, this is delicious hot or cold, so bring out the chopsticks and dig in!

Preparation time: 25 minutes

Preheat oven to 350°F (180°C)

Makes 4 servings

¼ cup	tamari	50 mL
¼ cup	balsamic vinegar	50 mL
2 tbsp	apple cider or juice	25 mL
2	cloves garlic, minced	2
8 oz	tempeh, cut into ½-inch (1 cm) cubes	250 g
8 oz	rice vermicelli noodles	250 g
¼ cup	fresh lemon juice	50 mL
3 tbsp	mirin	50 mL
2 tbsp	rice vinegar	25 mL
1 tbsp	toasted sesame oil	15 mL
1 tsp	hot pepper sauce	5 mL
4 cups	fresh spinach, washed and torn into bite-size pieces	1 L
1	sweet red pepper, diced	1
1 cup	sliced mushrooms	250 mL
Half	English cucumber, thinly sliced	Half
3	green onions, sliced	3

In bowl, combine tamari, rice vinegar, apple cider, garlic and ¼ cup (50 mL) water; add tempeh and stir to coat. Marinate for at least 10 to 30 minutes.

Transfer tempeh and any marinade to parchment paper-lined or nonstick baking sheet; bake in 350°F (180°C) oven for 8 minutes.

Meanwhile, bring 8 cups (2 L) water to boil. Place noodles in large bowl; pour boiling water over top. Let stand for 10 minutes or until al dente. Drain and cool under running water; drain well and return to bowl. Spoon tempeh and marinade over noodles.

In small bowl, combine lemon juice, mirin, vinegar, sesame oil and hot pepper sauce; pour over noodles. Place spinach on large platter; top with noodles. Arrange red pepper, mushrooms, cucumber and green onions on noodles.

Per serving: 434 calories · 20 g protein · 9 g total fat · 70 g carbohydrate · 3 g fibre (moderate)
· 1 g saturated fat · 0 mg cholesterol · 1070 mg sodium
· excellent source iron, vitamin C, folacin

Tempeh Burgers

━━ ━━ ━━

Burgers are a terrific way to showcase tempeh's remarkable texture. The addition of sautéed veggies, cooked rice and herbs creates a burger meal supreme. Serve with 100,000 Island Sauce (page 188).

Preparation time: 25 minutes
Makes 10 burgers

¼ cup	olive oil	50 mL
2	cloves garlic, minced	2
1	red onion, finely chopped	1
1	sweet green pepper, chopped	1
1	carrot, grated	1
1 tsp	soy sauce	5 mL
1 lb	finely chopped tempeh	500 g
2½ cups	cooked sushi rice (1 cup/250 mL raw)	625 mL
½ cup	dry bread crumbs	125 mL
2	eggs, lightly beaten	2
2 tbsp	chopped fresh dill	25 mL
1 tsp	salt	5 mL
¼ tsp	cayenne pepper	1 mL

In nonstick skillet, heat 2 tbsp (25 mL) of the oil over medium heat; cook garlic for 1 minute. Add onion; cook for 5 minutes or until softened. Add green pepper, carrot and soy sauce; cook for 3 minutes. Remove to large bowl; let cool for 5 minutes.

Add tempeh, rice, bread crumbs, eggs, dill, salt and cayenne; mix well. Using ½ cup (125 mL) measure, shape into 10 patties.

In skillet, heat 1 tbsp (15 mL) of the remaining oil over medium heat; cook burgers, in batches and using more oil if necessary, for 8 minutes, turning once, or until reddish brown.

Per serving: 253 calories · 12 g protein · 10 g total fat · 29 g carbohydrate · 1 g fibre · 2 g saturated fat · 43 mg cholesterol · 324 mg sodium · good source folacin

Versatile Sauces

The following sauces are almost like condiments. I often use them to add extra zip and tang to a meal, especially when I'm serving both kids and adults whose palates differ widely.

All-Purpose Sauce

Try this tangy sauce with rice, noodles or veggie burgers.

Preparation time: 30 minutes
Makes 3 cups (750 mL)

1½ cups	raisins	375 mL
¼ cup	apple cider vinegar	50 mL
2 tsp	chili flakes	10 mL
6	cloves garlic, halved	6
1 tsp	salt	5 mL
1	fresh red chili pepper, seeded and sliced	1
1 cup	canned whole tomatoes with juice	250 mL
¾ cup	plum or fruit jam	175 mL
½ cup	pineapple juice	125 mL
¼ cup	packed brown sugar	50 mL

In food processor, combine raisins, vinegar, chili flakes, garlic, salt, chili pepper and tomatoes; process until smooth. Transfer to saucepan along with jam, pineapple juice and brown sugar; bring to boil, stirring. Reduce heat and simmer for 20 minutes.

Per tbsp (15 mL): 37 calories · 0 g protein · 0 g total fat · 10 g carbohydrate · trace fibre · 0 g saturated fat · 0 mg cholesterol · 58 mg sodium

Sesame Seed Sauce

This thick sauce is best served with burgers and kebabs. Try it with Black Bean Quinoa Burgers (page 157) or Tofu Nuggets with Swiss Chard (page 166).

Preparation time: 10 minutes
Makes 1 cup (250 mL)

½ cup	sesame seeds	125 mL
1	clove garlic, crushed	1
½ tsp	chopped fresh gingerroot	2 mL
½ cup	water	125 mL
2 tbsp	soy sauce	25 mL
2 tbsp	extra virgin olive oil	25 mL
1 tbsp	kombu powder	15 mL
Pinch	red pepper flakes	Pinch

In small skillet, toast sesame seeds over medium-high heat for 4 minutes until golden brown and beginning to pop. In food processor or blender, process seeds, garlic and ginger until finely chopped.

Add water, soy sauce, oil, kombu powder and red pepper flakes; process until combined and thick. (Sauce can be refrigerated in airtight container for up to 1 week.)

Per tbsp (15 mL): 45 calories · 1 g protein · 4 g total fat · 1 g carbohydrate · 0 g fibre · 1 g saturated fat · 0 mg cholesterol · 141 mg sodium

Barbecue Sauce

This is great for basting tofu and tempeh. An excellent choice with Tempeh Burgers (page 184).

Preparation time: 10 minutes
Makes 1 cup (250 mL)

¼ cup	barley miso	50 mL
¼ cup	tomato paste	50 mL
¼ cup	grated onion	50 mL
¼ cup	apple cider vinegar	50 mL
¼ cup	maple syrup	50 mL
2	cloves garlic, minced	2
2 tbsp	olive oil	25 mL
½ tsp	dry mustard	2 mL
¼ tsp	allspice	1 mL

In bowl, whisk together miso, tomato paste, onion, vinegar, maple syrup, garlic, oil, mustard and allspice. (Sauce can be refrigerated in airtight container for up to 1 week; mix well before using.)

Per tbsp (15 mL): 42 calories · 1 g protein · 2 g total fat · 6 g carbohydrate · 1 g fibre · trace saturated fat · 0 mg cholesterol · 160 mg sodium

100,000 Island Sauce

Here is my version of the classic Thousand Island Dressing.

Preparation time: 5 minutes
Makes ½ cup (125 mL)

⅓ cup	mayonnaise	75 mL
2 tbsp	ketchup	25 mL
2 tsp	mellow white miso	10 mL
1 tsp	Dijon mustard	5 mL

In small bowl, whisk together mayonnaise, ketchup, miso and mustard until smooth. (Sauce can be refrigerated in airtight container for up to 1 week.)

Per tbsp (15 mL): 75 calories · trace protein · 7 g total fat · 2 g carbohydrate · 0 g fibre · 1 g saturated fat · 5 mg cholesterol · 158 mg sodium

6
Breakfasts, Muffins and Buns

Pecan Fruit Granola

Flax and Fruit Granola

Fruit Couscous

Breakfast Burrito

Kiwi and Banana Mini Pancakes

Soy Milk Shake

Breakfast Banana Smoothie

Strawberry Dream Freeze

Fruit Spread

Miso Apple Spread

Orange Poppy Seed Cranberry Muffins

Oatmeal Apple Muffins

Blueberry Muffins

Banana Nut Muffins

Dried Fruit and Brown Rice Muffins

Cameron's Favourite Muffins

Sticky Cinnamon Buns

Pecan Fruit Granola

━━ ━━ ━━

I love this granola topped with low-fat yogurt and fresh fruit. Or I often spoon it into a ripe cantaloupe half.

Preparation time: 5 minutes
Preheat oven to 350°F (180°C)
Cooking time: 15 minutes
Makes 4 servings

1½ cups	rolled oats	375 mL
½ cup	pecans, coarsely chopped	125 mL
2 tbsp	liquid honey	25 mL
½ cup	dried fruit (cranberries, cherries, dates or figs)	125 mL
¼ tsp	ground cardamom	1 mL

On small rimmed baking sheet, toast oats in 350°F (180°C) oven for 8 minutes. Stir in pecans; bake for 4 minutes.

Drizzle with honey; bake for 2 minutes. Spoon into large bowl. Stir in dried fruit and cardamom.

Per serving: 288 calories · 6 g protein · 12 g total fat · 42 g carbohydrate · 5 g fibre (high) · 1 g saturated fat · 0 mg cholesterol · 2 mg sodium

Flax and Fruit Granola

━━ ━━ ━━

Experts tell us that breakfast is the most important meal of the day. It can be the most delicious too when it's this crunchy granola served with yogurt or milk. I often eat the granola as a snack throughout the day. An excellent source of vitamin E, flax seeds are also rich in Omega-3 fatty acids and aid in the digestion of high-fibre foods, such as whole grains. Store flax seeds in the freezer because their high oil content makes them prone to rancidity.

Preparation time: 10 minutes

Preheat oven to 350°F (180°C)

Cooking time: 20 minutes

Makes 8 servings

½ cup	each sunflower and sesame seeds	125 mL
¼ cup	flax seeds	50 mL
2 cups	rolled oats	500 mL
¼ cup	coarsely chopped almonds	50 mL
½ tsp	each ground cinnamon and cardamom	2 mL
1 cup	mixed dried fruit (any combination of slivered apricots, figs, prunes, dates or dried cranberries, raisins, dried cherries)	250 mL

In clean coffee grinder, grind sunflower, sesame and flax seeds a little at a time. Place in large bowl; mix in oats, almonds, cinnamon and cardamom.

Spread mixture on large rimmed baking sheet. Toast in 350°F (180°C) oven, stirring twice, until golden, about 20 minutes. Stir in dried fruit; mix well. (Granola can be stored in airtight container for up to 2 weeks.)

Per serving: 285 calories · 10 g protein · 15 g total fat · 32 g carbohydrate · 6 g fibre (very high) · 2 g saturated fat · 0 mg cholesterol · 10 mg sodium · good source iron, folacin

Fruit Couscous

━━ ━━ ━━

My friend Kate Gammal contributed this little gem of a recipe. It is a big hit with my running friends who like the idea of combining grains and fruits for the energy it provides. Any combination of diced fruit will do, as long as it equals 4 cups (1 L).

Preparation time: 30 minutes

Makes 6 servings

3⅓ cups	fresh orange juice	825 mL
1 cup	couscous	250 mL
1 tsp	each ground ginger and cinnamon	5 mL
3	plums, pitted and diced	3
2	oranges, membranes removed and chopped	2
1	pear, cored and diced	1
1 cup	strawberries, diced	250 mL
¼ cup	chopped fresh mint	50 mL

In small saucepan, bring 1⅓ cups (325 mL) of the orange juice to boil. Stir in couscous; cover and remove from heat. Let stand for 5 minutes; fluff with fork. Turn out into serving bowl.

In another small saucepan, bring remaining orange juice, ginger and cinnamon to boil; reduce heat and simmer for about 20 minutes or until reduced to ½ cup (125 mL). Let cool.

Stir plums, oranges, pear, strawberries and mint into couscous. Pour cooled juice over couscous; toss until well combined.

Per serving: 243 calories · 6 g protein · 1 g total fat · 54 g carbohydrate · 4 g fibre (high)
· 0 g saturated fat · 0 mg cholesterol · 7 mg sodium
· excellent source vitamin C, folacin

Breakfast Burrito

Beans and dried fruit make a wonderful meal, especially first thing in the morning, says my husband, Jim, who enjoyed them for breakfast during his travels through Central and South America.

Preparation time: 20 minutes
Makes 4 servings

¼ cup	chopped dried apricots	50 mL
¼ cup	chopped dried apple	50 mL
¼ cup	dried cranberries	50 mL
¾ cup	apple juice	175 mL
1	cardamom pod, cracked	1
1	can (14 oz/398 mL) pinto beans, drained and rinsed	1
¼ tsp	salt	1 mL
4	10-inch (25 cm) flour tortillas	4

In medium saucepan, combine apricots, apple, cranberries, apple juice and cardamom; heat over low heat for 5 minutes.

Add beans and bring to boil. Reduce heat and simmer, uncovered and stirring often, for 8 to 10 minutes or until liquid has almost evaporated. Discard cardamom. Add salt.

In skillet, warm each tortilla over medium heat for 2 minutes, turning once. Place ½ cup (125 mL) filling down centre of each, leaving about 1 inch (2.5 cm) uncovered at bottom and top. Fold bottom and top over filling; fold sides over top.

Per serving: 338 calories · 10 g protein · 4 g total fat · 66 g carbohydrate · 8 g fibre (very high)
· 1 g saturated fat · 0 mg cholesterol · 670 mg sodium
· excellent source iron · good source folacin

Kiwi and Banana Mini Pancakes

─── ─── ───

These cute little pancakes are a great way to use up leftover cottage cheese. Feel free to substitute your favourite fruit. Serve with maple syrup.

Preparation time: 20 minutes

Makes about 15 mini pancakes

½ cup	cottage cheese	125 mL
¼ cup	plain yogurt	50 mL
1	egg	1
1 tsp	maple syrup	5 mL
¼ tsp	vanilla	1 mL
Pinch	salt	Pinch
½ cup	whole wheat flour	125 mL
½ tsp	baking powder	2 mL
1	kiwifruit, quartered lengthwise and sliced	1
1	small banana, halved lengthwise and sliced	1
2 tbsp	canola oil	25 mL

In food processor, combine cottage cheese, yogurt, egg, maple syrup, vanilla and salt; purée until smooth. Transfer to bowl.

In small bowl, combine flour and baking powder; stir into cottage cheese mixture until just combined. Gently stir in kiwifruit and banana.

In nonstick skillet, heat 1 tbsp (15 mL) of the oil over medium-high heat. Using 1 tbsp (15 mL) batter for each pancake, and remaining oil as necessary, drop batter onto skillet. Cook for 3 minutes or until bottom is golden and bubbles break on top but do not fill in. Turn and cook for 3 minutes or until bottom is golden brown.

Per pancake: 54 calories · 2 g protein · 2 g total fat · 6 g carbohydrate · 1 g fibre
· trace saturated fat · 15 mg cholesterol · 47 mg sodium

Soy Milk Shake

═ ═ ═

When breakfast-on-the-run truly means speed, here's a tasty solution.

Preparation time: 5 minutes
Makes 2 servings

1 cup	vanilla soy milk	250 mL
1 cup	frozen mixed berries	250 mL
½ cup	fresh orange juice	125 mL
¼ cup	quick-cooking rolled oats	50 mL
2 tbsp	good-tasting nutritional yeast	25 mL
4	ice cubes, crushed	4

In blender, blend soy milk with berries at high speed until smooth. Add orange juice, oats, yeast and ice; blend at high speed for about 1½ minutes or until ice has melted.

Per serving: 182 calories · 9 g protein · 5 g total fat · 31 g carbohydrate · 5 g fibre (high) · trace saturated fat · 0 mg cholesterol · 19 mg sodium · excellent source vitamin C, folacin · good source calcium

Breakfast Banana Smoothie

Freeze the bananas the night before to have them ready and waiting to make this drink.

Preparation time: 5 minutes

Makes 2 servings

2	large frozen bananas, peeled	2
1 cup	low-fat vanilla yogurt	250 mL
½ cup	fresh orange juice	125 mL
¼ cup	quick-cooking rolled oats	50 mL
2 tbsp	good-tasting nutritional yeast	25 mL
4	ice cubes, crushed	4
Dash	vanilla	Dash

In blender, combine bananas, yogurt, orange juice, oats, yeast, ice and vanilla; blend at high speed for about 1½ minutes or until ice has melted.

Per serving: 320 calories · 11 g protein · 6 g total fat · 64 g carbohydrate · 3 g fibre (moderate) · 2 g saturated fat · 7 mg cholesterol · 76 mg sodium · excellent source vitamin C, folacin · good source calcium

Strawberry Dream Freeze

With a rich, full flavour, this drink is a powerhouse of energy.

Preparation time: 5 minutes

Makes 2 servings

2 cups	frozen strawberries	500 mL
1½ cups	vanilla low-fat yogurt	375 mL
½ cup	vanilla soy milk	125 mL

In blender or food processor, blend together strawberries, yogurt and soy milk until smooth.

Per serving: 253 calories · 10 g protein · 5 g total fat · 46 g carbohydrate · 3 g fibre (moderate) · 2 g saturated fat · 10 mg cholesterol · 115 mg sodium · excellent source calcium, vitamin C · good source folacin

Fruit Spread

==== ==== ====

My version of jam, this spread is delicious on toast. This uses up that excess dried fruit you bought for granola.

Preparation time: 30 minutes

Makes 1 cup (250 mL)

2 cups	apple juice	500 mL
1 cup	dried fruit (cherries, cranberries, raisins or combination)	250 mL
2 tbsp	coarsely grated orange zest	25 mL
2 tbsp	coarsely grated lemon zest	25 mL
1 tbsp	rice syrup or liquid honey	15 mL
½ tsp	ground cinnamon	2 ml

In small saucepan, combine apple juice, dried fruit, orange and lemon zest, rice syrup and cinnamon. Simmer over low heat for 20 minutes or until fruit is tender.

Transfer to food processor fitted with metal blade; purée until smooth. Pour back into saucepan. Simmer for 10 minutes, stirring. Let cool. (Spread can be refrigerated in airtight container for up to 1 week.)

Per tbsp (15 mL): 41 calories · 0 g protein · 0 g total fat · 10 g carbohydrate · 1 g fibre · 0 g saturated fat · 0 mg cholesterol · 1 mg sodium

Miso Apple Spread

An unusual variation on *apple butter*.

Preparation time: 10 minutes
Makes ½ cup (125 mL)

1 cup	unsweetened applesauce	250 mL
3 tbsp	white miso	50 mL
2 tsp	rice syrup	10 mL

In skillet, whisk together applesauce, miso and rice syrup. Cook over low heat, stirring, for about 7 minutes or until thickened. Transfer to airtight container. (Spread can be refrigerated for up to 5 days.)

Per tbsp (15 mL): 31 calories · 1 g protein · trace total fat · 7 g carbohydrate · 1 g fibre · 0 g saturated fat · 0 mg cholesterol · 238 mg sodium

Orange Poppy Seed Cranberry Muffins

———

Using the right liquid ingredients will help keep muffins moist and tender.
Full-fat soy milk is a good stand-in for dairy milk but you can use either.

Preparation time: 15 minutes

Preheat oven to 350°F (180°C)

Cooking time: 25 minutes

Makes 12 muffins

¼ cup	poppy seeds	50 mL
1½ cups	unbleached white flour	375 mL
1½ cups	whole wheat pastry flour	375 mL
1 tbsp	baking powder	15 mL
½ tsp	salt	2 mL
1½ cups	vanilla soy milk	375 mL
½ cup	maple syrup	125 mL
⅓ cup	canola oil	75 mL
2 tbsp	finely grated orange zest	25 mL
¾ cup	dried cranberries	175 mL

Roast poppy seeds in nonstick skillet over medium heat for 3 minutes, stirring. Transfer to large bowl. Stir in white and whole wheat flours, baking powder and salt. Make well in centre.

In another bowl, whisk together soy milk, maple syrup, oil, orange zest and cranberries. Pour into well and stir just enough to moisten dry ingredients.

Spoon batter into 12 greased or paper cup-lined muffin cups, filling to top. Bake in 350°F (180°C) oven for 25 minutes or until cake tester inserted in centre comes out clean. Let cool in pan for 5 minutes; turn out onto wire racks and let cool.

Per muffin: 242 calories · 5 g protein · 8 g total fat · 39 g carbohydrate · 3 g fibre (moderate) · 1 g saturated fat · 0 mg cholesterol · 167 mg sodium

Oatmeal Apple Muffins

Kate Gammal's son, Alecko, loves to bake. After he informed me that a muffin with lots of rolled oats would be a big hit with six-year-olds, I developed this recipe.

Preparation time: 15 minutes

Preheat oven to 375°F (190°C)

Cooking time: 20 minutes

Makes 18 muffins

1½ cups	large-flake rolled oats	375 mL
¾ cup	unbleached white flour	175 mL
½ cup	whole wheat pastry flour	125 mL
2 tbsp	wheat germ	25 mL
1¼ tsp	baking soda	6 mL
1 tsp	ground cinnamon	5 mL
2	medium apples (unpeeled), coarsely grated	2
½ cup	raisins	125 mL
½ cup	sunflower seeds	125 mL
2 cups	buttermilk	500 mL
⅓ cup	liquid honey	75 mL
2 tbsp	butter, melted	25 mL
1	egg, lightly beaten	1

In food processor, finely chop oats; transfer to bowl. Add white and whole wheat flours, wheat germ, baking soda and cinnamon. Mix in apples, raisins and sunflower seeds. Whisk together buttermilk, honey, butter and egg; stir into dry ingredients until just moistened.

Spoon batter into 18 greased or paper cup-lined muffin cups, filling three-quarters full. Bake in 375°F (190°C) oven for 20 to 25 minutes or until cake tester inserted in centre comes out clean. Let cool in pans for 5 minutes; turn out onto wire rack and let cool.

Per muffin: 149 calories · 5 g protein · 4 g total fat · 24 g carbohydrate · 2 g fibre (moderate) · 1 g saturated fat · 16 mg cholesterol · 128 mg sodium

Blueberry Muffins

━━ ━━ ━━

Every August we buy lots of wild blueberries from a roadside farm in southern Ontario. Tiny but incredibly sweet, they also freeze well—perfect for baking these berries-in-every-bite treats any time of year.

Preparation time: 10 minutes
Preheat oven to 350°F (180°C)
Cooking time: 25 minutes
Makes 12 muffins

1½ cups	unbleached white flour	375 mL
1½ cups	whole wheat pastry flour	375 mL
1 tbsp	baking powder	15 mL
1 tsp	salt	5 mL
½ cup	maple syrup	125 mL
⅓ cup	canola oil	75 mL
3 tbsp	plain yogurt	50 mL
1¼ cups	vanilla soy milk	300 mL
2 cups	fresh or frozen blueberries	500 mL

In large bowl, mix together white and whole wheat flours, baking powder and salt. Make well in centre. In another bowl, whisk together maple syrup, oil and yogurt until creamy; whisk in soy milk. Pour into well and stir just enough to moisten dry ingredients.

Spoon 1 tbsp (15 mL) batter into each of 12 paper cup-lined muffin cups. Spoon 1 tbsp (15 mL) blueberries onto each. Stir remaining blueberries into remaining batter; spoon evenly over blueberries.

Bake in 350°F (180°C) oven for 25 minutes or until cake tester inserted in centre comes out clean. Let cool in pan for 10 minutes; turn out onto wire racks and let cool.

Per muffin: 218 calories · 4 g protein · 7 g total fat · 36 g carbohydrate · 3 g fibre (moderate) · 1 g saturated fat · 0 mg cholesterol · 265 mg sodium

Banana Nut Muffins

Baking without eggs can be a challenge, but it can be done. Grinding flax seeds and blending them with water (1 tbsp/15 mL ground flax dissolved in 3 tbsp/45 mL water equals 1 egg) results in a consistency similar to egg whites. It binds the ingredients and produces a very good muffin. The banana and molasses complement the slightly nutty flavour of the ground flax seeds.

Preparation time: 10 minutes

Preheat oven to 375°F (190°C)

Cooking time: 15 minutes

Makes 12 muffins

2 cups	whole wheat pastry flour	500 mL
1 cup	wheat germ or oat bran	250 mL
2 tsp	each baking powder and ground cinnamon	10 mL
1 tsp	allspice	5 mL
½ tsp	baking soda	2 mL
1 cup	mashed bananas (about 2 ripe bananas)	250 mL
1 cup	milk (non-dairy or dairy)	250 mL
⅓ cup	canola oil	75 mL
1	egg (or 2 egg whites)	1
¼ cup	each Barbados molasses and maple syrup	50 mL
½ cup	chopped dates	125 mL
½ cup	coarsely chopped pecans or walnuts	125 mL

In large bowl, mix together flour, wheat germ, baking powder, cinnamon, allspice and baking soda. In another bowl, whisk together bananas, milk, oil, egg, molasses and maple syrup. Stir into dry ingredients until just moistened. Stir in dates and pecans.

Spoon batter into 12 large greased muffin cups, filling to top. Bake in 375°F (190°C) oven for 15 to 20 minutes or until cake tester inserted in centre comes out clean. Let cool in pan for 5 minutes; turn out onto rack and let cool.

Tip: In recent years the selection of non-dairy milk products has expanded tremendously. You can drink them as a beverage, use them in baked goods, cream sauces or puddings, whenever dairy milk is called for. Once opened, store in the refrigerator and use within a week or before expiry date.

Per muffin: 267 calories · 6 g protein · 12 g total fat · 38 g carbohydrate · 5 g fibre (high) · 1 g saturated fat · 18 mg cholesterol · 104 mg sodium · good source iron

Dried Fruit and Brown Rice Muffins

These muffins are chewy, sweet and light. Choose your favourite fruit or use any combination of dried cranberries, blueberries, cherries, apples, prunes, apricots, dates and figs for these wholesome muffins.

Preparation time: 15 minutes
Preheat oven to 400°F (200°C)
Cooking time: 25 minutes
Makes 12 muffins

1½ cups	whole wheat pastry flour	375 mL
1 cup	unbleached white flour	250 mL
¼ cup	rolled oats	50 mL
1 tbsp	baking powder	15 mL
½ tsp	salt	2 mL
1½ cups	vanilla soy milk	375 mL
½ cup	canola oil	125 mL
½ cup	maple syrup	125 mL
2 cups	cooked brown rice	500 mL
1 cup	mixed dried fruit, coarsely chopped	250 mL

In large bowl, mix together whole wheat and white flours, rolled oats, baking powder and salt. In another bowl, stir together soy milk, oil and maple syrup; stir in brown rice and dried fruit. Stir into dry ingredients until just moistened.

Spoon into 12 large paper cup-lined muffin cups. Bake in 400°F (200°C) oven for 25 minutes or until cake tester inserted in centre comes out clean. Let cool in pan for 10 minutes; turn out onto rack and let cool.

Per muffin: 284 calories · 5 g protein · 10 g total fat · 45 g carbohydrate · 4 g fibre (high) · 1 g saturated fat · 0 mg cholesterol · 169 mg sodium

Cameron's Favourite Muffins

━━ ━━ ━━

Cameron, my sports-loving son, loves muffins. He added walnuts, oranges, raisins and butter to this recipe and declared these the best muffins ever.

Preparation time: 15 minutes

Preheat oven to 350°F (180°C)

Cooking time: 40 minutes

Makes 12 muffins

2 cups	whole wheat pastry flour	500 mL
1 tbsp	baking powder	15 mL
2 tsp	ground cinnamon	10 mL
½ tsp	allspice	2 mL
¼ tsp	sea salt	1 mL
½ cup	raisins or chopped dried fruit	125 mL
½ cup	walnuts or pecans, chopped	125 mL
	Grated zest and chopped pulp of 2 oranges	
2	eggs	2
1 cup	vanilla soy milk	250 mL
½ cup	liquid honey	125 mL
¼ cup	butter, melted	50 mL
1 tsp	vanilla	5 mL

In large bowl, mix together flour, baking powder, cinnamon, allspice and salt. Add raisins, nuts, orange zest and chopped orange. Make well in centre. In another bowl, mix together eggs, soy milk, honey, butter and vanilla. Pour into well and stir together until blended and runny.

Spoon into 12 paper cup-lined muffin cups; place pan on baking sheet in case any batter spills over. Bake in 350°F (180°C) oven for 40 minutes or until slightly browned. Let cool in pan for 5 minutes; turn out onto rack and let cool.

Per muffin: 231 calories · 5 g protein · 9 g total fat · 37 g carbohydrate · 4 g fibre (high) · 3 g saturated fat · 46 mg cholesterol · 167 mg sodium

Sticky Cinnamon Buns

Marilyn Crowley, Associate Food Editor at **Chatelaine**, is a terrific chef, food writer and pillar of support and good taste in my culinary travels. I have always enjoyed her recipe for sticky cinnamon buns, which are moist and chewy.

Preparation time: 1¼ hour

Preheat oven to 350°F (180°C)

Cooking time: 30 minutes

Makes 12 rolls

3 cups	unbleached white flour (approx.)	750 mL
¼ cup	granulated sugar	50 mL
2 tbsp	milk	25 mL
1 tbsp	instant yeast	15 mL
¾ tsp	salt	4 mL
¾ cup	very warm water	175 mL
¾ cup	very thick unsweetened applesauce	175 mL
3	egg whites	3
1½ cups	whole wheat flour	375 mL
FILLING:		
⅔ cup	packed brown sugar	150 mL
1 tbsp	ground cinnamon	15 mL
2 tsp	ground cardamom	10 mL
1 tbsp	butter, softened	15 mL
¾ cup	raisins	175 mL
¼ cup	liquid honey	50 mL

In large bowl, stir together 1 cup (250 mL) of the white flour, sugar, milk, yeast and salt until evenly mixed. Stir in water and applesauce. Stir in egg whites, whole wheat flour and 1 cup (250 mL) white flour. Add remaining white flour, ¼ cup (50 mL) at a time, until dough is firm enough to form into ball.

Turn out onto floured surface. Knead, adding up to 1 cup (250 mL) more flour as neccessary, for about 10 minutes or until dough is smooth and elastic. Cover with greased waxed paper then damp tea towel; let rest for 10 minutes.

Filling: In small bowl, stir together brown sugar, cinnamon and cardamom. Turn dough out onto lightly floured surface; roll out dough into 18- x 12-inch (45 x 30 cm) rectangle. Thinly spread butter over surface, leaving 1-inch (2.5 cm) border on one long side uncovered. Sprinkle with sugar mixture and raisins. Drizzle with honey.

Beginning at long edge with filling, roll up jelly-roll style, sealing bare edge to roll by pinching. Cut crosswise into 12 equal rounds. Place, cut side down and slightly apart, in greased 13- x 9-inch (3.5 L) cake pan. Cover and let rise until doubled in size, about 45 minutes.

Bake in 350°F (180°C) oven for about 30 minutes or until golden. Let cool in pan on rack for 5 minutes; invert onto plate.

Tip: Instant yeast is widely available in supermarkets. It's also known as quick-rising yeast.

Per rolls: 304 calories · 7 g protein · 2 g total fat · 68 g carbohydrate · 4 g fibre (high) · 1 g saturated fat · 3 mg cholesterol · 176 mg sodium · good source iron, folacin

7
Sweet Endings

Citrus Pecan Quick Bread

Pumpkin Spice Bread

Poppy Seed Banana Bread

Pecan Pear Coffee Cake

Double Yogurt Chocolate Cake and Icing

Chocolate Tofu Cheesecake for Nonbelievers

Tofu Brownies

Fruit Juice Bars

Fruit Nut Bars

Crispy Rice Nut Butter Squares

Mackenzie's Crunchy Almond Oatmeal Cookies

Apricot Almond Biscotti

Autumn Fruit Crisp

Pumpkin Pie with Tofu

Mango Cream Pie

Berry Pie with Nut Crust

Quinoa Pudding

Apple Strawberry Kanten

Banana Redwood Logs

Mango Banana Pops

Citrus Pecan Quick Bread

———

This fast and easy loaf has a refreshing citrus flavour. I prefer to use organic oranges. Their flavour is more pronounced and I think they are also juicier and sweeter.

Preparation time: 15 minutes
Preheat oven to 350°F (180°C)
Cooking time: 45 minutes
Makes 1 loaf, 8 slices

¼ cup	butter, vegetable oil or soy margarine	50 mL
½ cup	liquid honey	125 mL
2	eggs	2
¼ cup	fresh orange juice	50 mL
1 tsp	vanilla	5 mL
2 cups	whole wheat pastry flour	500 mL
1 tbsp	baking powder	15 mL
¼ tsp	salt	1 mL
½ cup	chopped pecans	125 mL
1 tbsp	grated orange zest	15 mL

In bowl, cream butter; beat in honey until smooth and creamy. Beat in eggs. Add orange juice and vanilla; beat until well blended.

In separate bowl, combine flour, baking powder and salt; stir into wet ingredients. Fold in pecans and orange zest. Pour into greased 8- x 4-inch (1.5 L) loaf pan; smooth top.

Bake in 350°F (180°C) oven for 45 minutes or until cake tester inserted in centre comes out clean. Let cool in pan for 10 to 15 minutes; turn out onto rack and let cool completely. (Loaf can be wrapped and refrigerated for up to 3 days.)

Per slice: 279 calories · 6 g protein · 12 g total fat · 40 g carbohydrate · 4 g fibre (high) · 4 g saturated fat · 69 mg cholesterol · 245 mg sodium

Pumpkin Spice Bread

＝ ＝ ＝

Chewy, fragrant and moist, this is a delicious snacking cake.

Preparation time: 15 minutes
Preheat oven to 325°F (160°C)
Cooking time: 1 hour
Makes 1 loaf, 8 slices

1 cup	raisins	250 mL
½ cup	apple juice	125 mL
2 cups	unbleached white flour	500 mL
½ cup	whole wheat pastry flour	125 mL
½ cup	wheat germ	125 mL
1½ tsp	baking powder	7 mL
1 tsp	baking soda	5 mL
1 tsp	each ground cinnamon and ginger	5 mL
½ tsp	salt	2 mL
¼ tsp	ground cloves	1 mL
1	can (14 oz/398 mL) pumpkin purée or 1¾ cups (425 mL) homemade	1
½ cup	maple syrup	125 mL
2	eggs	2

In small saucepan, bring raisins and apple juice to boil; remove from heat and let cool.

In large bowl, mix together white and whole wheat flours, wheat germ, baking powder, baking soda, cinnamon, ginger, salt and cloves. In another bowl, whisk together pumpkin, maple syrup and eggs; stir into dry ingredients until just blended. Stir in raisin mixture.

Spread batter in greased 8- x 4-inch (1.5 L) loaf pan; bake in 325°F (160°C) oven for 1 hour or until cake tester inserted in centre comes out clean. Let cool in pan for 10 minutes; turn out onto rack and let cool.

Per slice: 255 calories · 7 g protein · 2 g total fat · 54 g carbohydrate · 4 g fibre (high) · 1 g saturated fat · 43 mg cholesterol · 291 mg sodium · good source iron

---

Poppy Seed Banana Bread

—— ▬ ▭ ▬ ——

Fresh banana bread is a staple dessert in my home. Adding poppy seeds to the recipe makes me feel as if I've gone to Europe for tea and cake.

Preparation time: 15 minutes
Preheat oven to 325°F (180°C)
Cooking time: 50 minutes
Makes 1 loaf, 10 slices

1½ cups	unbleached white flour	375 mL
½ cup	whole wheat pastry flour	125 mL
⅓ cup	poppy seeds	75 mL
2 tsp	baking powder	10 mL
1 tsp	baking soda	5 mL
½ tsp	salt	2 mL
3	ripe bananas, mashed (about 1 cup/250 mL)	3
½ cup	packed brown sugar	125 mL
½ cup	unsweetened applesauce	125 mL
3	egg whites	3
1 tsp	vanilla	5 mL

In large bowl, mix together white and whole wheat flours, poppy seeds, baking powder, baking soda and salt. In another bowl, whisk together bananas, brown sugar, applesauce, egg whites and vanilla; stir into dry ingredients until just blended.

Spread batter in greased 9- x 5-inch (2 L) loaf pan; bake in 325°F (180°C) oven for 50 to 60 minutes or until cake tester inserted in centre comes out clean. Let cool in pan for 10 minutes; turn out onto rack and let cool.

Per serving: 232 calories · 6 g protein · 3 g total fat · 46 g carbohydrate · 2 g fibre (moderate) · trace saturated fat · 0 mg cholesterol · 381 mg sodium · good source iron

Pecan Pear Coffee Cake

═ ═ ═

My friend Liz Greisman enjoys cake of any kind. One day she brought some
overripe pears from her garden and we created this first-class treat.

Preparation time: 15 minutes

Preheat oven to 375°F (190°C)

Cooking time: 40 minutes

Makes 1 cake, 10 servings

½ cup	pecans	125 mL
⅓ cup	packed brown sugar	75 mL
2 tbsp	butter	25 mL
2 tbsp	almond butter	25 mL
1 tsp	ground cardamom	5 mL
	CAKE:	
½ cup	butter or soy margarine, softened	125 mL
½ cup	maple syrup	125 mL
2	eggs	2
1 tsp	vanilla	5 mL
½ tsp	almond extract	2 mL
2 cups	unbleached white flour	500 mL
1 tsp	ground cardamom	5 mL
1 tsp	baking powder	5 mL
¼ tsp	each baking soda and salt	1 mL
⅓ cup	low-fat plain yogurt	75 mL
1	large pear, peeled, cored and chopped	1

In food processor fitted with metal blade, chop pecans. Add sugar, butter, almond butter and cardamom; pulse until combined. Set aside.

Cake: In large bowl, cream butter; beat in maple syrup until blended. Beat in eggs, one at a time. Beat in vanilla and almond extract. In small bowl, sift together flour, cardamom, baking powder, baking soda and salt; add to butter mixture in two additions alternately with yogurt, being careful not to overmix. Stir in pear.

Spread batter in greased 9-inch (2.5 L) square cake pan. Cover evenly with pecan mixture. Bake in 375°F (190°C) oven for 40 minutes or until cake tester inserted in centre comes out clean.

Per serving: 391 calories · 6 g protein · 21 g total fat · 46 g carbohydrate · 2 g fibre (moderate) · 9 g saturated fat · 83 mg cholesterol · 281 mg sodium · good source iron

Double Yogurt Chocolate Cake
and Icing

━━ ━━ ━━

Once the cycle of children's birthday parties begins, a chocolate cake with icing is the preferred choice. This one is always a hit.

Preparation time: 20 minutes

Preheat oven to 350°F (180°C)

Cooking time: 35 minutes

Makes 1 cake, 10 servings

3 oz	unsweetened chocolate, chopped	90 g
2 tbsp	finely ground coffee granules	25 mL
⅓ cup	boiling water	75 mL
1½ cups	unbleached white flour	375 mL
1 tsp	baking soda	5 mL
1 tsp	each ground cinnamon and cardamom	5 mL
½ tsp	each baking powder and salt	2 mL
1 cup	plain 2% yogurt	250 mL
1 tsp	vanilla	5 mL
1 cup	liquid honey	250 mL
½ cup	canola oil	125 mL
2	eggs	2
ICING:		
8 oz	bittersweet chocolate, chopped	250 g
1 cup	plain 2% yogurt	250 mL

In top of double boiler over gently simmering water, melt chocolate; let cool. Stir coffee granules into boiling water; let cool.

In small bowl, mix together flour, baking soda, cinnamon, cardamom, baking powder and salt; set aside. In separate bowl, combine yogurt, coffee and vanilla; set aside.

In large bowl, beat together honey, oil and eggs. Beat in cooled chocolate until blended. Beat in flour mixture alternately with yogurt mixture.

Divide batter between 2 greased and floured 8-inch (1.2 L) round cake pans. Bake in 350°F (180°C) oven for 30 to 35 minutes or until top springs back when touched lightly. Let cool before removing from pans.

Icing: In top of double boiler over gently simmering water, melt chocolate; let cool for 10 minutes. Stir in yogurt until smooth. Let cool for 30 minutes or until slightly thickened and spreadable.

Spread some of the icing over top of one of the cake layers. Top with remaining cake layer. Spread remaining icing over top and sides.

Per serving: 469 calories · 9 g protein · 26 g total fat · 60 g carbohydrate · 4 g fibre (high)
· 9 g saturated fat · 46 mg cholesterol · 295 mg sodium
· good source iron

Chocolate Tofu Cheesecake
for Nonbelievers

To test this recipe I assembled a cheesecake tasting panel: Seamus Flaim, a fifteen-year-old cheesecake connoisseur, Laurie Malabar, a 20-year vegetarian veteran, Barbara Barron, an expert baker and Mackenzie Urquhart, a seven-year-old cheesecake lover. The verdict: absolutely delicious. The combination of almond nut butter, delicate, white miso, bananas and cocoa gives this cheesecake a slightly sweet taste with a firm texture. The perfect recipe for asking the "Guess what's in this?" question. Serve it topped with sliced kiwifruit or berries.

Preparation time: 15 minutes

Preheat oven to 350°F (180°C)

Cooking time: 55 minutes

Makes 12 servings

2 cups	graham cracker crumbs	500 mL
¼ cup	maple syrup	50 mL
2 tbsp	apple juice	25 mL
2 tbsp	canola oil	25 mL
	FILLING:	
1 lb	firm tofu, rinsed	500 g
2	bananas, quartered	2
1 cup	maple syrup	250 mL
½ cup	vanilla soy milk	125 mL
½ cup	almond nut butter	125 mL
⅓ cup	cocoa powder	75 mL
1 tbsp	each fresh lemon juice and vanilla	15 mL
1 tbsp	white miso	15 mL

In bowl, stir together crumbs, maple syrup, juice and oil; press onto bottom of lightly greased 9-inch (2.5 L) springform pan. Bake in 350°F (180°C) oven for 10 minutes. Let cool.

Filling: Rinse tofu and cut into quarters. In food processor, purée tofu until smooth. Add bananas, maple syrup, soy milk, almond butter, cocoa, lemon juice, vanilla and miso; blend until very smooth. Pour over crust. Bake for 55 minutes in 350°F (180°C) oven or until cake tester comes out clean. Let cool completely. To serve, cut with serrated knife.

Per serving: 304 calories · 7 g protein · 13 g total fat · 45 g carbohydrate · 2 g fibre (moderate) · 2 g saturated fat · 0 mg cholesterol · 201 mg sodium · good source iron

Tofu Brownies

This is the most tested recipe in the whole book because I kept trying to approximate a perfect brownie texture without using granulated sugar. I tried maple syrup, honey, Sucanat and rice syrup, but it was with sugar that the flavour and texture were in harmony. Prunes and tofu add a delicious—and healthy—dimension.

Preparation time: 20 minutes
Preheat oven to 350°F (180°C)
Cooking time: 45 minutes
Makes 24 brownies

2 tbsp	fresh lemon juice	25 mL
2 cups	vanilla soy milk	500 mL
2 cups	unbleached white flour	500 mL
2 cups	cocoa powder	500 mL
2 cups	granulated sugar	500 mL
2 tsp	each baking powder and baking soda	10 mL
½ tsp	salt	2 mL
1½ cups	dried pitted prunes	375 mL
1 tbsp	packed brown sugar	15 mL
8 oz	firm tofu, rinsed and quartered	250 g
2 tsp	vanilla	10 mL
½ cup	coarsely chopped pecans	125 mL

Add lemon juice to soy milk; set aside. In large bowl, stir together flour, cocoa, sugar, baking powder, baking soda and salt; set aside.

In another bowl, pour 1 cup (250 mL) boiling water over prunes; let soak for 10 minutes.

In food processor, purée together prunes, ¼ cup (50 mL) soaking liquid and brown sugar until a smooth paste. Add tofu and vanilla; purée until smooth. Add 1 cup (250 mL) of the soy milk mixture; blend well. Add to dry ingredients in two additions alternately with remaining soy milk, mixing well with wooden spoon after each. Stir in pecans.

Spread batter evenly in lightly greased 13- x 9-inch (3.5 L) cake pan. Bake in 350°F (180°C) oven for 45 minutes. Let cool on rack. Cut into squares.

Per serving: 185 calories · 4 g protein · 4 g total fat · 37 g carbohydrate · 5 g fibre (high) · 1 g saturated fat · 0 mg cholesterol · 226 mg sodium

Fruit Juice Bars

Lots of dried fruit on a granola base makes a chewy and filling treat. Use your favourite dried fruit.

Preparation time: 15 minutes

Preheat oven to 350°F (180°C)

Cooking time: 20 minutes

Makes 12 bars

2½ cups	granola	625 mL
½ cup	apple juice	125 mL
4 cups	dried chopped fruit	1 L
½ cup	apple or strawberry juice	125 mL
¼ cup	arrowroot flour	50 mL
1 tbsp	vanilla	15 mL
1 tsp	ground cardamom	5 mL

In food processor, grind granola until coarse; transfer to large bowl. Mix in apple juice. Press firmly over bottom of greased 13- x 9-inch (3.5 L) baking dish.

In food processor, process together dried fruit, juice, arrowroot, vanilla and cardamom for 3 minutes or until puréed. Spread evenly over granola crust.

Bake in 350°F (180°C) oven for 20 minutes. Let cool; cut into bars. (Bars can be refrigerated in airtight container for up to 5 days.)

Per bar: 237 calories · 3 g protein · 5 g total fat · 48 g carbohydrate · 5 g fibre (high) · 0 g saturated fat · 0 mg cholesterol · 22 mg sodium

Fruit Nut Bars

My athletic friend Geraldine Lyn-Piluso, captain of a football team, ate some of these bars before a practice and said she had an energy-inspired workout. They are a terrific alternative to the commercial energy bars. Instead of 2 eggs, you can substitute 2 tbsp (25 mL) ground flax seeds mixed with 6 tbsp (90 mL) water.

Preparation time: 20 minutes
Preheat oven to 350°F (180°C)
Cooking time: 50 minutes
Makes 18 squares

1 cup	whole wheat pastry flour	250 mL
1 cup	chopped pistachios	250 mL
½ cup	chopped dried figs	125 mL
½ cup	chopped dried prunes	125 mL
½ cup	chopped pitted dates	125 mL
½ cup	chopped dried apricots	125 mL
¼ cup	raisins	50 mL
¼ cup	canola oil	50 mL
1 tbsp	vanilla	15 mL
1 tsp	ground cinnamon	5 mL
2	eggs, lightly beaten	2
1	can (14 oz/398 mL) unsweetened, crushed pineapple, drained	1

In large bowl, mix together flour, pistachios, figs, prunes, dates, apricots and raisins. In separate bowl, mix together oil, vanilla, cinnamon, eggs and pineapple; pour into dry ingredients and mix thoroughly.

Spread batter evenly in greased 13- x 9-inch (3.5 L) baking dish. Bake in 350°F (180°C) oven for 50 minutes or until firm and slightly golden. Let cool to room temperature; cut into squares. (Squares can be refrigerated in airtight container for up to 5 days.)

Per square: 165 calories · 4 g protein · 8 g total fat · 22 g carbohydrate · 4 g fibre (high)
· 1 g saturated fat · 24 mg cholesterol · 9 mg sodium

Crispy Rice Nut Butter Squares

A very tasty snack that's my alternative to the popular mass-produced square.

Preparation time: 30 minutes

Makes 12 squares

½ cup	smooth almond nut butter	125 mL
½ cup	rice syrup	125 mL
½ cup	liquid honey	125 mL
1 tsp	vanilla	5 mL
½ cup	dried apricots, chopped	125 mL
½ cup	raisins	125 mL
½ cup	chopped almonds, toasted	125 mL
¼ cup	each sunflower and sesame seeds, toasted	50 mL
2½ cups	rice crisp cereal	625 mL
1¼ cups	rolled oats	300 mL

In large saucepan, heat together almond-nut butter, rice syrup, honey and vanilla over medium-low heat until blended.

Add apricots, raisins, almonds, sunflower and sesame seeds; mix well. Add rice crisp cereal and oats; mix to coat.

Using lightly oiled hands, press mixture evenly into greased 8-inch (2 L) square cake pan. Let stand for 15 minutes or until firm. Cut into squares.

Per square: 308 calories · 6 g protein · 13 g total fat · 46 g carbohydrate · 3 g fibre (moderate) · 1 g saturated fat · 0 mg cholesterol · 76 mg sodium · good source iron

Mackenzie's Crunchy Almond Oatmeal Cookies

━━ ━━ ━━

Kids love cookies, and my daughter, Mackenzie, is no exception. These treats earned unanimous approval from her Grade Two testing panel.

Preparation time: 10 minutes

Preheat oven to 400°F (200°C)

Cooking time: 12 minutes

Makes 28 cookies

2 cups	rolled oats	500 mL
1½ cups	unbleached white flour	375 mL
½ cup	packed brown sugar	125 mL
2 tsp	each baking powder and ground cinnamon	10 mL
1 tsp	ground cardamom	5 mL
¼ cup	crunchy almond nut butter	50 mL
¼ cup	butter, softened	50 mL
2	eggs	2
1 tsp	vanilla	5 mL
½ cup	apple cider	125 mL
½ cup	raisins	125 mL

In food processor fitted with metal blade, combine 1 cup (250 mL) of the oats, flour, sugar, baking powder, cinnamon and cardamom; process until coarsely ground. Stir in remaining oats.

In large bowl, cream together almond butter and butter. Beat in eggs and vanilla. Beat in apple cider. Stir in oat mixture until well blended. Stir in raisins.

Drop batter by tablespoonfuls (15 mL) onto nonstick baking sheets. Bake in 400°F (200°C) oven for 12 to 15 minutes or until golden. Let cool on rack. (Cookies can be stored in airtight container for up to 5 days.)

Per cookie: 108 calories · 3 g protein · 4 g total fat · 17 g carbohydrate · 1 g fibre · 1 g saturated fat · 20 mg cholesterol · 42 mg sodium

Apricot Almond Biscotti

━━ ━━ ━━

My friend Laura Buckley, who has been a pastry chef in upscale restaurants, was a good choice to test many of my "alternative" desserts because she was open-minded and knew what the perfect texture and taste should be. She was amazed at the flavour that organic ingredients added to the recipe. Of course, regular apricots and oranges will do too, but for that special taste, choose organic.

Preparation time: 30 minutes

Preheat oven to 325°F (160°C)

Cooking time: 1 hour

Makes 24 biscotti

	Juice and grated zest of 1 medium orange	
¾ cup	dried apricots	175 mL
1½ cups	whole wheat soft flour	375 mL
½ cup	Sucanat or packed brown sugar	125 mL
½ tsp	baking powder	2 mL
½ tsp	each ground cinnamon and cardamom	2 mL
¼ tsp	baking soda	1 mL
¼ tsp	ground nutmeg	1 mL
1	egg	1
1	egg white	1
½ cup	lightly toasted almonds, chopped	125 mL

In small saucepan, heat orange juice with apricots just until hot. Remove from heat; let stand for 20 minutes or until softened. Drain and reserve orange juice. Coarsely chop apricots.

In large bowl, sift together flour, sugar, baking powder, cinnamon, cardamom, baking soda and nutmeg. Make well in centre. In separate bowl, whisk together egg, egg white, orange zest and 1 tbsp (15 mL) reserved orange juice; gently stir into dry mixture until combined, adding more juice if necessary to make dough moist. Stir in almonds and apricots.

Transfer dough to parchment paper-lined baking sheet. With lightly floured hands, press into 16- x 2-inch (40 x 5 cm) log. Bake in 325°F (160°C) oven for 25 minutes. Let cool for 10 minutes on rack.

Reduce heat to 300°F (150°C). Cut log diagonally into about ½ inch (1 cm) thick slices. Stand on baking sheet, leaving space between each. Bake until light brown and crunchy, about 20 minutes. Let cool thoroughly on rack. (Biscotti can be stored in airtight container for up to 1 week.)

Per tbsp (15 mL): 72 calories · 2 g protein · 2 g total fat · 13 g carbohydrate · 1 g fibre · trace saturated fat · 9 mg cholesterol · 25 mg sodium

Autumn Fruit Crisp

—— ☐☐☐☐☐☐ ——

Take advantage of harvest time for this fruity dessert, but of course you can make it any time of year. It's wonderful served with yogurt.

Preparation time: 20 minutes

Preheat oven to 350°F (180°C)

Cooking time: 40 minutes

Makes 6 servings

4	large apples	4
4	ripe pears	4
1 cup	blueberries (fresh or frozen)	250 mL
¼ cup	apple-strawberry juice	50 mL
1 tbsp	arrowroot flour	15 mL
1 tsp	sea salt	5 mL
1 tsp	cardamom	5 mL
1 cup	rolled oats	250 mL
½ cup	pistachios, finely chopped	125 mL
¼ cup	whole wheat pastry flour	50 mL
2 tsp	canola oil	10 mL

Halve and core apples and pears, peeling if desired; thinly slice and place in bowl. Add blueberries, juice, arrowroot, salt and cardamom; toss to combine. Transfer to 8-cup (2 L) casserole dish.

In separate bowl, mix together oats, pistachios, flour and oil; sprinkle evenly over fruit. Bake in 350°F (180°C) oven for 40 minutes or until topping is crisp and golden brown. Serve warm.

Per serving: 316 calories · 6 g protein · 9 g total fat · 60 g carbohydrate · 10 g fibre (very high) · 1 g saturated fat · 0 mg cholesterol · 386 mg sodium · good source iron

---

Pumpkin Pie with Tofu

This delicious pie takes only 10 minutes to make, provided your crust is ready and waiting. Pumpkin is the best medium for tofu, and with the addition of ginger, allspice and molasses, you have all the traditional flavour with a dairy-free filling. Instead of this pie crust, you could also use the one from Chocolate Tofu Cheesecake for Nonbelievers (see page 220).

Preparation time: 10 minutes
Preheat oven to 350°F (180°C)
Cooking time: 1 hour
Makes 8 servings

8 oz	firm tofu, rinsed	250 g
2 cups	pumpkin purée	500 mL
1 cup	Barbados molasses	250 mL
1 tsp	ground cardamom	5 mL
1 tsp	vanilla	5 mL
½ tsp	each ground ginger, allspice and salt	2 mL
1	unbaked 9-inch (23 cm) pie crust	1

In food processor, purée tofu until smooth. Add pumpkin, molasses, cardamom, vanilla, ginger, allspice and salt; blend until creamy.

Pour filling into pie crust. Bake in 350°F (180°C) oven for 1 hour. Let cool on rack.

Per serving: 238 calories · 4 g protein · 7 g total fat · 43 g carbohydrate · 1 g fibre
· 2 g saturated fat · 0 mg cholesterol · 257 mg sodium
· good source calcium, iron

Mango Cream Pie

─ ─ ─

This dairy-free, rich and delicious pie sets beautifully thanks to two ingredients, agar-agar and kudzu.

Preparation time: 25 minutes

Setting time: 1 hour

Makes 8 servings

1½ cups	graham cracker crumbs	375 mL
¼ cup	maple syrup	50 mL
2 tbsp	canola oil	25 mL
	FILLING:	
1 tbsp	kudzu	15 mL
2 cups	vanilla soy milk	500 mL
3 tbsp	agar-agar flakes	50 mL
3 tbsp	maple syrup	50 mL
	Grated zest of 1 small orange	
Pinch	each cardamom and sea salt	Pinch
½ tsp	vanilla	2 mL
2	small or 1 large very ripe mango, peeled and puréed	2

In bowl, mix together graham cracker crumbs, maple syrup and oil; evenly press onto bottom and up side of 9-inch (23 cm) pie plate. Set aside.

Filling: In small bowl, dissolve kudzu in 2 tbsp (25 mL) of the soy milk; set aside. In saucepan, combine remaining soy milk, agar-agar, maple syrup, orange zest, cardamom and salt; bring to boil. Reduce heat and simmer for 5 minutes.

Add dissolved kudzu; cook, stirring constantly, until thickened enough to coat back of wooden spoon. Add vanilla. Fold in puréed mango; stir for 1 minute or until combined. Remove from heat. Pour filling into crust. Refrigerate for 1 hour or until set. (Pie can be covered and refrigerated for up to 3 days.)

Per serving: 177 calories · 3 g protein · 5 g total fat · 32 g carbohydrate · 2 g fibre (moderate) · 1 g saturated fat · 0 mg cholesterol · 118 mg sodium

Berry Pie with Nut Crust

━━ ━━ ━━

Nut crusts are one of my favourites. Chewy and filling, they complement any kind of berry well.

Preparation time: 50 minutes

Preheat oven to 350°F (180°C)

Setting time: 45 minutes

Makes 8 servings

¾ cup	rolled oats	175 mL
½ cup	almonds, pecans or walnuts	125 mL
¾ cup	whole wheat pastry flour	175 mL
½ cup	unsweetened coconut	125 mL
½ tsp	sea salt	2 mL
½ tsp	ground cardamom	2 mL
⅓ cup	canola oil	75 mL
⅓ cup	maple syrup	75 mL
1 tsp	vanilla	5 mL
	FILLING:	
1 cup	apple-strawberry juice	250 mL
5 tbsp	agar-agar flakes	75 mL
2 cups	fresh or frozen berries	500 mL
1 tbsp	fresh lemon juice	15 mL
1 tsp	vanilla	5 mL
Pinch	sea salt	Pinch
1 tbsp	kudzu	15 mL
¼ cup	cold water	50 mL

In food processor, grind rolled oats with nuts into coarse meal; transfer to bowl. Stir in flour, coconut, salt and cardamom. Add oil, maple syrup and vanilla; mix well. Press into greased 9-inch (23 cm) pie plate to make about ¼-inch (5 mm) thick base and slightly thicker side. Prick 5 times with fork to prevent buckling. Bake in 350°F (180°C) oven for 20 minutes or until slightly golden. Let cool for 10 minutes before filling.

Filling: Meanwhile, in saucepan, simmer apple-strawberry juice and agar-agar flakes for 10 minutes, stirring often. Add berries, lemon juice, vanilla and salt. Reduce heat to low.

Dissolve kudzu in 2 tbsp (25 mL) cold water; stir into berry mixture until sauce is clear and shiny. Simmer for 3 minutes. Transfer to bowl; let cool for 20 minutes. Spoon into crust, spreading evenly. Refrigerate for 45 minutes or until set. (Pie can be refrigerated for up to 5 days.)

Per serving: 242 calories · 4 g protein · 14 g total fat · 27 g carbohydrate · 3 g fibre (moderate) · 4 g saturated fat · 0 mg cholesterol · 122 mg sodium · good source vitamin C

Quinoa Pudding

━━ ━━ ━━

This mock rice pudding recipe has fruit, nuts and aromatic spices to show-case quinoa's creamy texture and delicious flavour. Quinoa is a nutrient-rich grain that is slightly sweet and can be easily seasoned. 1¼ cups (300 mL) raw quinoa cooked in 2½ cups (625 mL) water equals 3 cups (750 mL) cooked quinoa.

Preparation time: 15 minutes
Preheat oven to 350°F (180°C)
Cooking time: 40 minutes
Makes 8 servings

3 cups	cooked quinoa	750 mL
2 cups	vanilla soy milk	500 mL
2 cups	raspberries (fresh or frozen)	500 mL
½ cup	raisins	125 mL
⅓ cup	maple syrup	75 mL
2	eggs, beaten	2
1 tsp	grated lemon zest	5 mL
½ cup	chopped pistachios	125 mL
½ tsp	each ground cardamom and cinnamon	2 mL
¼ tsp	ground nutmeg	1 mL

In large bowl, combine cooked quinoa, soy milk, raspberries, raisins, maple syrup, eggs and lemon zest; stir just until combined. Pour into greased 8-inch (2 L) square baking dish.

Combine pistachios, cardamom, cinnamon and nutmeg; sprinkle over top. Bake in 350°F (180°C) oven for 40 minutes or until liquid is absorbed. Serve warm or cold.

Per serving: 273 calories · 9 g protein · 8 g total fat · 45 g carbohydrate · 5 g fibre (high) · 1 g saturated fat · 54 mg cholesterol · 31 mg sodium · excellent source iron

Apple Strawberry Kanten

This is Japanese Jello, a totally vegetarian gelatin made from agar-agar seaweed. You can vary the fruit juice to suit your taste and the fresh berries, fruit and nuts to go with it, too.

Preparation time: 20 minutes

Chilling time: 2 hours

Makes 6 servings

3 cups	apple-strawberry juice	750 mL
¼ cup	agar-agar flakes	50 mL
½ cup	smooth almond nut butter	125 mL

In saucepan, simmer juice and agar-agar over medium-high heat for 5 minutes. Bring to boil; reduce heat and simmer for 15 minutes, stirring often. Pour into bowl; refrigerate until firm, 1½ to 2 hours.

Transfer to food processor. Add nut butter; process until smooth and creamy. Pour into individual serving cups. Refrigerate until cold. (Kanten can be refrigerated for up to 5 days.)

Per serving: 197 calories · 3 g protein · 12 g total fat · 21 g carbohydrate · 1 g fibre · 1 g saturated fat · 0 mg cholesterol · 8 mg sodium · excellent source vitamin C

Banana Redwood Logs

This was my kids' favourite snack when they were younger. Often, I left out the Popsicle™ stick and let them eat these frozen delights with their hands. Roll the banana in any kind of nut you like if you don't have pecans on hand.

Preparation time: 5 minutes

Freezing time: 3 hours

Makes 4 servings

2	bananas	2
2 tbsp	each fresh lemon juice and maple syrup	25 mL
3 tbsp	finely chopped pecans	50 mL

Peel and halve bananas. Insert Popsicle™ stick into end of each.

In shallow bowl, combine lemon juice and maple syrup; roll bananas in mixture to coat. In separate bowl, roll bananas in pecans. Place on plate lined with waxed paper; freeze for 3 hours.

Per serving: 113 calories · 1 g protein · 4 g total fat · 21 g carbohydrate · 1 g fibre · trace saturated fat · 0 mg cholesterol · 2 mg sodium

Mango Banana Pops

━━ ━━ ━━

Lots of kids don't like the look of figs but enjoy the taste of them. This is a terrific easy dessert for kids but everyone in my family enjoys them. You can vary the juice (papaya, guava, pineapple) for a refreshing treat on a hot summer's day.

Preparation time: 5 minutes

Freezing time: 4 hours

Makes 8 servings

¾ cup	mango juice	175 mL
½ cup	fresh orange juice	125 mL
2	bananas	2
2	figs	2

In blender or food processor, blend together mango and orange juices, bananas and figs until smooth. Pour into 8 molds; freeze for 4 hours.

Per serving: 57 calories · 1 g protein · 0 g total fat · 14 g carbohydrate · 1 g fibre · 0 g saturated fat · 0 mg cholesterol · 1 mg sodium

GLOSSARY

Adzuki beans: Small, dark red beans used in traditional Japanese cuisine. Easily digestible.

Agar-agar (*see also* kudzu): A flavourless vegetarian jelling agent made from sea vegetables, sold in the form of flakes or bars. It dissolves easily without lumping and sets at room temperature or, for a shorter setting time, in the refrigerator.

Amaranth: Principal food of the Aztecs. A little yellow seed high in protein and calcium. It releases a starchy substance during cooking and has a gelatinous quality. I like to use amaranth flour and will often substitute up to ¼ cup (50 mL) of it for the same amount of whole wheat pastry flour.

Apple cider vinegar: An inexpensive, fruity-tasting vinegar that needs refrigeration if unpasteurized. Its low level of acidity (4%) with a hint of sweetness means that it's wonderful for use in salad dressings.

Arame: A mild-flavoured, thinly sliced sea vegetable resembling black angel hair pasta when sold in precooked dried form. Used in soups, salads and casseroles and is easy to prepare. Arame's sweet taste is due to the presence of mannitol, a noncaloric sugar which is present in many brown algae.

Arborio rice: Used in the northern Italian meal risotto, these short, plump, starchy grains swell with liquid but don't become mushy when properly cooked. Do not rinse the rice before cooking in order not to wash away the starch that gives it a creamy texture. Also, cook uncovered because it absorbs water quickly.

Arrowroot flour: An easily digested starch often used in babyfoods and convalescent diets. Arrowroot is used for last-minute thickening when the cook wants a clear sauce with no floury aftertaste, which makes it a good substitute for cornstarch. Dissolve arrowroot in cold water or cooled cooking liquid to make a smooth paste before heating. It will thicken at a relatively low temperature. Use 1 tbsp (15 mL) arrowroot for each 1 cup (250 mL) liquid. Stir the paste gradually into soups or sauces. Do not overcook once thickened.

Balsamic vinegar: A northern Italian vinegar made from white Trebbiano grape juice that becomes deep amber when aged in wood barrels, often for 10 years.

Barley: Whole barley has a pleasant, chewy texture, a very satisfying, earthy taste and is easy to digest. Pot barley has nutritional advantages over the refined or pearl barley that has had its hard outer layers removed.

Basmati rice: A variety of long-grain rice that has a delicate aroma and nutlike taste that suits many cuisines. White basmati rice is parboiled and cooks in 20 minutes. Brown basmati rice cooks in 45 minutes.

Beet greens: These greens taste a lot like spinach and shrink considerably during cooking. They are very perishable, so use within two days. When left attached to beets, the greens will last longer. Trim off the stems and coarsely chop any large leaves after rinsing. Stems can be boiled and sautéed longer than leaves.

Black beans: Small oval beans with mild taste and robust texture. Readily absorb the flavours of chilies and spices.

Buckwheat: Originally from China and Siberia, buckwheat has a strong earthy flavour and is very porous, so it cooks fast. Wash raw buckwheat groats quickly otherwise they absorb water and lose their shape. I dry-roast buckwheat first to improve its texture, making it firmer and crunchier. When you combine an egg with the uncooked groats, the egg albumen helps the buckwheat retain its shape.

Bulgur wheat: Made from wheat berries that have been steamed, dried and crushed to create small brown gritty pieces. My choice for best texture is medium ground bulgur. Add measured boiling water to bulgur and cover. Fifteen minutes later, the grain should have absorbed the water and be ready to use. Never rinse bulgur because it will turn to mush.

Brown rice: Short-grain brown rice has a reputation for chewiness and good texture. Brown rice is available in long- , medium- and short-grain types. The size has no bearing on nutrition, only on the texture after cooking. The longer the grain, the more separate and fluffy the rice.

Brown rice syrup: A very mild sweetener made by adding sprouted, dried barley to cooked rice, which ferments and breaks down into sugars.

Brown rice vinegar: A light-amber-coloured vinegar with a pleasant flavour. Used in Asian cooking because of its subtle (4 percent) acidic properties, it combines well with oils and herbs to create tasty dressings and marinades.

Canola oil: Extracted from rapeseed, canola oil is clear, with little colour. It is lower in saturated fat than any other oil and contains cholesterol-lowering omega-3 fatty acids. I like to use it for baking and stir-frying.

Celeriac: A tough knobby root resembling parsley and celery in flavour.

Chickpeas: Small, round legumes with a tip and creamy beige colour. A staple food in the Middle East and used to make hummus. Also known as garbanzo beans.

Chili peppers: Available both fresh and dried, chili peppers range in taste from mild to hot, hot, hot! The heat is in the seeds and surrounding membranes, so removing them reduces the heat. Their volatile oils can cause a lot of discomfort if you touch your mouth or eyes when preparing chilies. Protect yourself by wearing thin rubber gloves and wash your hands in hot soapy water after handling. Some terrific chilies to use are jalapeño, chipotle or ancho.

Chili powder: Chili powder is made from a blend of ground chilies that vary in heat. Often cumin, oregano and salt are added to the mixture. Flavour fades within six months, so buy it in small amounts.

Cilantro: Cilantro looks like Italian parsley, but has longer leaves and a unique taste and smell. It's also known as coriander and Chinese parsley. Store fresh cilantro in the fridge, stems down, in a container of water. Cover the leaves with a wet cloth secured with an elastic band or use a plastic bag. It should last for five days.

Coconut milk: Made by soaking shredded fresh coconut in hot water. When using canned coconut milk, make sure you mix the thin liquid at the top with the bottom, creamy, thick layer. Refrigerate leftovers for a maximum of three days.

Cornmeal flour: Dried corn ground into a coarse flour. Used to make polenta.

Curry paste: A paste made of chilies and other spices different from Indian curry powders. You can purchase prepared yellow, red and green Thai curry pastes at health food stores, Asian markets and specialty stores.

Curry powder: Curry powders range from a mixture of three ingredients to seventeen. The most common ingredients are cumin, mustard seeds, red chilies, black pepper and turmeric. You can roast and crush the seeds yourself or buy prepared blends. Use within six months.

Dill: Dill is easy to recognize with its lacy, feathery green leaves. It can be stored in the fridge, roots in a container of water, covered by plastic wrap or a wet cloth, for five days. Add it at the end of cooking because its flavour is affected by heat.

Extra virgin olive oil: Made from the first pressing of olives. The lighter the colour of the oil, the more delicate the flavour. The natural acidity of extra virgin olive oil cannot exceed 1 percent.

Flax seeds: Store these glossy brown seeds in the freezer. Grinding them improves their digestibility. They are an excellent source of vitamin E and omega-3 fatty acids and also make a good replacement for eggs in baking. One egg equals 1 tbsp (15 mL) ground flax seeds mixed with 3 tbsp (45 mL) water; wait for 5 minutes then add to wet ingredients.

Good-tasting nutritional yeast: Not to be confused with baking yeast, this good-tasting nutritional yeast is not a leavening agent but a condiment that is added to sauces, casseroles and salads for its nutritional value and cheeselike flavour. You can find it in health food stores under the brand name Vegetarian Support Formula (T-6635+) Primary Grown Nutritional Yeast, made by Red Star Yeast and Products.

Great Northern beans: Large white beans used in chili, soups, stews and dips.

Hijiki: A seaweed that resembles black angel hair spaghetti and is high in calcium and iron. Hijiki means "bearer of wealth and beauty" in Japanese.

Honey: Made by bees from the nectar they collect from flowers. There are many types of honey, such as alfalfa, clover, orange blossom and buckwheat. Honey is a liquid sweetener and will attract moisture, keeping baked goods from going stale too quickly. Cakes and pies made with honey tend to be chewy rather than crispy. Honey does not require refrigeration. The sugar in honey may crystallize but this will not affect its quality.

Kanten: A basic pudding made from either fruit juice or non-dairy milk and agar-agar, a jelling agent.

Kale: This dark green leafy vegetable may have either curly or flat leaves and has a pleasant flavour. It should not be eaten raw.

Kidney beans: These versatile kidney-shaped beans can either be red or white. They tend to hold their shape during prolonged periods of cooking and so are often used in stews and soups.

Kombu: A seaweed often used as a soup and stock base. A strip of kombu cooked with water releases glutamic acid and mineral salts. Glutamic acid is the natural version of that dubious flavouring agent monosodium glutamate (MSG).

Kudzu (*see also* agar-agar): One of the world's largest vegetable roots, averaging 175 lb (79 kg) and reaching up to 7 feet (2.13 m) in length. Kudzu is a cooking starch with no overpowering taste and is sold in small chunks, which need to be crushed with a mortar and pestle before measuring. Dissolve the measured amount of kudzu in the measured amount of liquid to add to other ingredients as an excellent thickening agent. It can be combined with agar-agar and jells fruit purées particularly well.

Lemongrass: A herb with a lemon-flavoured, delicate scent. Use the bottom of the lemongrass but discard the part where the woody stem begins.

Lentils: Small, lens-shaped seeds that come in many colours (green, red, orange and brown) and sizes. They do not need to be soaked before cooking. My favourite is a French variety called Lentille Puys. They are sweet, retain their shape and are terrific in salads. Hulled lentils used in Indian cuisine (dal) cook more quickly.

Maple syrup: Made from boiling the sap of maple trees; 40 litres of sap is reduced 1 litre of syrup. It is graded according to colour, flavour and thickness. Grade A is a particular favourite because of its delicate flavour.

Millet: A tiny yellow grain that is quite bland, so combine it with flavourful ingredients. Toast millet before cooking; it browns easily and releases a pleasant aroma. High in protein and B vitamins.

Mirin: A sweet, low-alcohol wine used for cooking. The alcohol evaporates upon contact with heat. Like sake, mirin is made with a mixture of rice koji (bacterial culture), cooked white rice and water. It is thick, sweet and pale golden. It is supposed to balance the saltiness in other soy foods, such as miso and soy sauce.

Miso: A salty paste made by cooking and fermenting soybeans and grains (see pages 7 and 8). Unpasteurized miso has better flavour and nutritional value but must be refrigerated.

Molasses: A strong-flavoured thick, dark liquid that remains after sucrose has been removed from sugar cane. Use it for baking and in sauces. My favourite type is Barbados molasses, made from the first press of the sugar cane.

Navy beans: Small, white beans used in soups, stews and salads and for baked beans.

Nori: Thin black sheets of seaweed with a briny flavour. Used for wrapping sushi rolls and also as a garnish when cut into thin strips or shredded. I love crumpled nori sprinkled on popcorn!

Oats: Unlike other grains, only the hull is removed when oats are milled. The germ and bran remain in the edible portion. The hulled whole grain, known as the groat, is the cornerstone for all the oat cereals sold. You can buy Irish or Scotch oats in this form. Rolled oats are made by slicing the groats, then steaming them, rolling them into flakes and drying them. This allows them to cook quickly.

Pine nuts: These delicious nuts are very expensive because they are harvested from pine cones on the trees. They are very perishable and need to be refrigerated.

Pinto beans: Brown beans with a creamy texture. Used a lot in burritos, chili and other refried bean dishes.

Pistachio nuts: These have a green kernel and are available in plain beige shells, salted and unsalted, usually roasted. Grated, pistachios make an elegant garnish.

Quinoa: Quinoa is about the size of a sesame seed and is a nutritional powerhouse. Also available as quinoa flour. Quinoa must be rinsed in a fine-mesh sieve under cold running water for at least five minutes or until the water runs clear to remove all the bitter saponin coating. Bring water or stock to a boil before adding the rinsed quinoa.

Rice vermicelli: Dried noodle that comes in a variety of thicknesses. Widely available in supermarkets.

Rice vinegar: Made from fermented rice wine, this is a light, honey-coloured, sweetish vinegar with a mild acidity level of 4 percent.

Soybeans: A major source of protein in China and Japan for thousands of years. Easy to grow, nutritious and extremely versatile. Soybeans are used to make tofu, miso and tempeh.

Soy milk: A nondairy beverage derived from cooked, strained soybeans. The taste varies depending on oil and sweetener content. Drink it chilled. Comes in various flavours; I've used either original or vanilla-flavoured in this book. You can substitute dairy milk for soy milk in any of the recipes.

Soy sauce: This salty sauce is made from soybeans mixed with a bacterial culture and a grain—usually cracked roasted wheat. This mixture is fermented and salted and left to age for up to two and a half years. The soy sauce is then strained and bottled.

Spelt flour: One of the ancient grains, spelt is a strain of wheat. It has a texture similar to standard wheat but has a different genetic profile. Many people with wheat sensitivities find they have a tolerance for spelt. It can be substituted for whole wheat flour (soft or pastry).

Split peas: Skinned and available as green and yellow, they require no soaking and cook quickly, especially in soups.

Sucanat: The dehydrated juice of organically grown sugar cane in granular form. It is very expensive.

Sushi rice: This is white rice that has rice vinegar and mirin added to the cooking water so the end result is a lightly sweetened vinegared white rice that is slightly sticky.

Swiss chard: White-ribbed and red chard are the two kinds readily available. To use the stems, trim the tops and bottoms, then peel off the tough fibres that cover the stalk, which I often braise. The leaves can be boiled or steamed and used to stuff, or coarsely chopped and added to soups near the end of cooking, or layered in a casserole. Rinse well, store in fridge in plastic bag for three days.

Tahini: This paste is made from calcium-rich ground sesame seeds. It's used in hummus, a chickpea spread. Store in the fridge and stir before use.

Tamari: A type of soy sauce made from soybeans, salt and bacterial culture but without the cracked roast wheat. Make sure you read the labels carefully when you are buying tamari. Good quality tamari or soy sauce contains no preservatives, food colouring or sugar.

Tamarind paste: A concentrated paste made from the tart pulp of the tamarind fruit. Sold in Indian and Asian stores.

Teff: The grain of Ethiopia. An extremely tiny seed that is high in calcium and protein. I use it mixed with other grains or grind the seeds to make flour.

Tempeh: Made from fermenting crushed, cooked soybeans. See pages 6 to 7.

Toasted sesame oil: Extracted from toasted sesame seeds, this oil has a wonderful aroma. It's excellent in marinades, salad dressings and sauces and drizzled onto cooked pasta and casserole dishes.

Tofu (also firm tofu, pressed tofu and frozen tofu): Made from soybean curds. See pages 4 to 6.

Triticale flour: A new strain of grain, triticale is a mix of wheat and rye. It is low in gluten and needs to be combined with whole wheat flour for baking.

Umeboshi plum vinegar: Bright, purple-pink, salty, sour vinegar made from the liquid that surfaces from pickled umeboshi plums or apricots. It goes very well with mirin and toasted sesame oil.

Unbleached white flour: White flour is made from the starchy endosperm (interior starchy kernel) of the grain, without any fibre or the germ's vital nutrients. When it is first produced, white flour is creamy coloured, and as it ages, the flour whitens and is known as unbleached white flour.

Wheatgerm: Found in the germ layer of whole wheat kernels, it contains B vitamins, vitamin E and insoluble fibre. It can go rancid quickly due to its high oil content so it needs to be refrigerated and used within two weeks. Keep in a sealed container to retain moisture and prevent odour absorption.

Whole wheat flour (hard): The wheat used to make hard whole wheat flour is high in gluten, which assists bread to expand and hold its shape. It is also more coarsely milled and therefore has more bran.

Whole wheat flour (soft or pastry): Finely ground, it is made from a softer wheat that is lower in protein but contains some of the bran and germ. It is used for cakes and pastries.

Wild rice: Wild rice expands to three times its volume during cooking. (That justifies its expensive price.) It is slim, black and has a nutty taste and aroma. It isn't really a rice either: it's the seed of an aquatic grass from Canada and the United States. I like to cook it alone, then combine it with other grains.

Wine vinegars: Stronger than grain-based vinegars with 6 to 7 percent level of acidity. The deeper the colour, the stronger the flavour, and the more pronounced the taste and ability of the vinegar to flavour the food or dressing. Wine vinegars are made from red or white wines and range from mild to strong in taste, often depending on the type of wine and length of fermentation.

BIBLIOGRAPHY

━━ ━━ ━━

It is by no means complete, but here is a list of books that have inspired me in the search for terrific vegetarian cuisine.

Alford, Jeffrey and Naomi Duguid. **Seductions of Rice**. Toronto: Random House of Canada, 1998.

Belleme, John and Jan. **Culinary Treasures of Japan**. Garden City, N.Y.: Avery, 1992.

Bloodroot Collective. **The Perennial Political Palate**. Bridgeport, Conn.: Sanguinaria, 1993.

Estella, Mary. **Natural Foods Cookbook**. Tokyo: Japan Publications, 1985.

Goldbeck, Nikki and David. **American Wholefoods Cuisine**. New York: New American Library, 1983.

Goldstein, Darra. **The Vegetarian Hearth**. New York: HarperCollins, 1996.

Jordan, Julie. **Wings of Life**. Trumansberg, N.Y.: Crossing Press, 1976.

Langton, Brenda and Margaret Stuart. **The Café Brenda Cookbook**. Stillwater, MN: Voyageur Press, 1992.

Madison, Deborah. **The Savory Way**. New York, N.Y.: Bantam Books, 1990.

Polden, Rodney and Pamela Thornley. **Salt Spring Island Cooking**. Toronto: Macmillan, 1993.

Raichlen, Steven. **High-Flavour Low-Fat Vegetarian Cooking**. New York: Viking Penguin, 1995.

Sass, Lorna. Lorna Sass' **Short-cut Vegetarian**. New York: William Morrow, 1997.

Shulman, Martha Rose. **Fast Vegetarian Feasts**. New York: Doubleday, 1982.

Shurtleff, William and Akiko Aoyagi. **The Book of Tempeh**. New York: Harper and Row, 1979.

Wood, Rebecca. **The Splendid Grain**. New York: William Morrow, 1997.

INDEX

Grilled Tofu, 132
Tempeh Kebabs, 178

H

Herbs, 13–14. *See also individual herbs.*
Hijiki, 12
    ingredient in: main course, 174; salads, 89, 94; soups, 50, 52, 54, 63
    Hijiki with Carrots and Sesame Seeds, 123
Honey
    ingredient in: buns, 208; cake, 218; muffins, 202, 207; quick bread, 213; side dish, 133; squares, 226

J

Jalapeño peppers
    ingredient in: main courses, 157, 160; side dish, 127; soup, 60
Japanese eggplant
    ingredient in: main courses, 142, 162, 180; soup, 67
    Japanese Eggplant with Miso and Curry Paste, 146
Jim's Slaw with Tofu Sour Cream, 86

K

Kanten, Apple Strawberry, 237
Kebabs, Tempeh, 178
Kidney beans, 9
Kiwifruit
    Kiwi and Banana Mini Pancakes, 195
    Mango Kiwi Salsa, 45
Kombu, 12
    ingredient in: side dish, 126; soups, 52, 63, 64, 68; spread, 38
    Kombu Orange Rice, 125

L

Lasagna, Tofu, 168
Latkes, Vegetable, 28
Leeks
    ingredient in: main courses, 137, 144, 170; side dish, 120; soups, 49, 52, 68, 70
    Leek, Parsnip and Quinoa Soup, 66
    Potato, Leek and Asparagus Soup, 64
    Tofu with Leeks and Peanut Butter, 167
Lemongrass
    Chickpea Miso Soup with Chilies and Lemongrass, 60
Lentils
    Aunt Jenny's Split Pea and Lentil Soup, 54
    Black Olive Salad with Lentils and Feta, 90
    Carrot Lentil Soup, 50
    cooking, 9
    Curried Lentil Soup, 65
    ingredient in: salad, 96
    Lentil Pistachio Loaf, 158
    Lentil Spinach Salad, 102
Lettuce
    ingredient in: main course, 150; salads, 77, 80, 90
    Spinach and Lettuce Salad with Goat Cheese, 78
Linguine Salad with Ginger and Garlic, 89
Loaves
    Lentil Pistachio Loaf, 158
    Tamarind Tempeh Buckwheat Loaf, 180

Mushroom Pepper Bruschetta, 21
Mushroom Veggie Broth, 51
Mustard Curry Salad Dressing, 110

N

Nachos, 27
Natural food, definition of, 15
Navy beans
    cooking, 9
    Navy Bean Pâté, 26
Non-dairy milk products, 205
Nori, 12
    ingredient in: appetizer, 24
    Stuffed Nori Trumpets, 22
Nuts, 13. *See also individual nuts.*
    Banana Nut Muffins, 204
    Berry Pie with Nut Crust, 234
    Fruit Nut Bars, 225

O

Oats
    ingredient in: dessert, 230; drinks,
        196, 197; granola, 191, 192;
        muffins, 206; pie, 234; squares,
        226
    Mackenzie's Crunchy Almond
        Oatmeal Cookies, 227
    Oatmeal Apple Muffins, 202
Oils, 14
Olives
    Black Olive Salad with Lentils
        and Feta, 90
    ingredient in: salad, 98; snack, 35;
        soup, 67
    olive oil, 14
    Tofu Olive Spread, 40
Omelettes, additions to, 127

Onions
    ingredient in: appetizers and snacks,
        28, 29; dip, 41; main courses,
        148, 150, 158, 168, 174, 176;
        salads, 92; side dishes, 115, 123,
        127, 130; soups, 50, 54, 57, 58,
        59, 61, 62, 63, 65
Onions, red
    ingredient in: main courses, 138,
        142, 147, 154, 156, 157, 160,
        162, 164, 171, 178, 184; salads,
        77, 78, 79, 82, 90, 91, 93, 96,
        99, 101, 102, 104; side dishes,
        122, 124, 126; soups, 49, 66,
        67, 71
    Soba Noodles with Red Onions,
        Black Beans and Kale, 140
Onions, Spanish
    ingredient in: main course, 152;
        soup, 57
Oranges, 213
    Citrus Pecan Quick Bread, 213
    ingredient in: couscous, 193;
        muffins, 207; salads, 77, 84
    juice, ingredient in: appetizer, 32;
        couscous, 193; dessert, 239;
        drinks, 196, 197; side dish, 117
    Kombu Orange Rice, 125
    Orange Garlic Miso Tempeh, 173
    Orange Poppy Seed Cranberry
        Muffins, 201
Oregano Salad Dressing, 106
Organic fruits and vegetables, 15–16

P

Pancakes, Kiwi and Banana Mini, 195
Pantry, organizing of, 16–18

Parmesan cheese
  ingredient in: appetizers and snacks,
    21, 31, 34, 35, 36; main courses,
    144, 168, 176; salad, 80; side
    dish, 124; soup, 61; spread, 39
Parsley
  ingredient in: appetizers and
    snacks, 28, 32; main courses,
    137, 144, 158, 170; pesto, 52;
    salad, 82; soups, 49, 50, 51, 61,
    62, 67, 68, 70
Parsnips, 137
  Curried Parsnip and Bean Burgers,
    152
  ingredient in: main course, 137;
    soup, 68
  Leek, Parsnip and Quinoa Soup, 66
Pastas
  additions to, 132
  Baked Tempeh and Rice Noodle
    Salad with Hot Sauce, 182
  ingredient in: soup, 61
  Linguine Salad with Ginger and
    Garlic, 89
  Mackenzie's Pasta Salad, 98
  Soba Noodles with Red Onions,
    Black Beans and Kale, 140
  Tofu Lasagna, 168
Pâté, Navy Bean, 26
Peanut butter
  Tofu with Leeks and Peanut
    Butter, 167
Pears
  ingredient in: couscous, 193;
    dessert, 230; salad, 77; side
    dishes, 118, 133
  Pecan Pear Coffee Cake, 216

Peas. *See* Green peas; Split peas.
Pecans
  ingredient in: brownies, 222;
    dessert, 238; muffins, 204, 207;
    pie, 234
  Citrus Pecan Quick Bread, 213
  Pecan Fruit Granola, 191
  Pecan Pear Coffee Cake, 216
Peppers, sweet
  Bean and Pepper Pie, 160
  ingredient in: appetizers and
    snacks, 21, 35; main courses,
    142, 147, 154, 160, 162, 164,
    167, 168, 176, 178, 180, 182,
    184; salads, 78, 79, 89, 93, 96,
    101, 104; side dishes, 115, 130;
    soups, 50, 56, 57, 60, 63, 67
  Mushroom Pepper Bruschetta, 21
  Roasted Pepper and Chickpea
    Dip, 37
  roasting peppers, 37
  Tri-Colour Peppers Stuffed with
    Chickpeas, Mint and Pine Nuts,
    148
Pesto, Sea Vegetable Chowder with,
  52
Pies
  dessert
    Berry Pie with Nut Crust, 234
    Mango Cream Pie, 232
    Pumpkin Pie with Tofu, 231
  savory
    Bean and Pepper Pie, 160
    Sweet Potato Celeriac Pie, 138
Pineapple
  ingredient in: bars, 225; salsa, 45
  Pineapple Beet Salad, 104

NOTES

New Vegetarian Basics

New Vegetarian Basics

New Vegetarian Basics